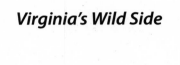

Virginia's Wild Side

Virginia's Wild Side

Fifty Outdoor Adventures from the Mountains to the Ocean

Curtis J. Badger

Illustrations by Vladimir Gavrilovic

UNIVERSITY OF VIRGINIA PRESS
Charlottesville and London

University of Virginia Press
© 2003 by Curtis J. Badger
Printed in the United States of America on acid-free paper
First published 2003

9 8 7 6 5 4 3 2 1

LIBRARY OF CONGRESS CATALOGING-IN-PUBLICATION DATA

Badger, Curtis J.
   Virginia's wild side : fifty outdoor adventures from the
mountains to the ocean / Curtis J. Badger ; illustrations by
Vladimir Gavrilovic.
      p.   cm.
   ISBN 0-8139-2162-7 (cloth : alk. paper)
   1. Outdoor recreation—Virginia—Guidebooks.
   2. Recreation areas—Virginia—Guidebooks.
   3. Virginia—Guidebooks. I. Title.
   GV191.42.V8 B33 2003
   796.5'09755—dc21

                                        2002012300

To Lynn and Tom, who have shared with me many of the adventures described here and have made them infinitely more enjoyable

Contents

Tidewater, the Middle Peninsula, and the Northern Neck

Central Virginia and the Highlands

Acknowledgments

Many people and organizations have helped make this book possible. I am especially indebted to the *Virginian-Pilot* newspaper of Norfolk, Virginia, which for several years now has put me in the enviable position of writing about places and activities that interest me. I would especially like to thank my editor there, David Simpson, who has been very supportive and has given me free rein to write about everything from salamander hunts to chopping firewood. Many of the accounts in this book began life as "Get Active!" features in the *Virginian-Pilot*.

I grew up on Virginia's Eastern Shore and have known that area well for a long time. I needed some help in getting to know other parts of the state. The staff of the Virginia Division of State Parks went out of their way to introduce me to places I probably never would have found on my own. Virginia's state parks were voted best in the nation as this book was going to press, and I can easily understand why. Not only are they clean, well-run public resources, but the staff and volunteers who keep them going are friendly, helpful, and knowledgeable.

I attended Emory and Henry College in southwest Virginia, and I enjoyed getting back to that beautiful part of the state to see what I had missed when I spent four years there in the pursuit of higher learning, along with other less-noble ventures. I would like to thank the Abingdon office of the Nature Conservancy of Virginia, Gregory

McConnell of my alma mater, Tom Horsch of Adventure Damascus, and Phoebe Cartright of Blue Blaze Shuttle.

Bill and Katherine Cochran introduced our family to several wonderful places in the Roanoke area and to an amazing hiker named Olen Waldrip, whose story is included here. Thanks also to Blane Chocklett, an extraordinary fisherman and guide.

Patty Long of the Northern Neck Tourism Council and Annette Bareford of the Virginia Division of State Parks showed me eagles along the Potomac River, fossils at Westmoreland, and a gold mine at Lake Anna. Botanist and river guide Garrie Rouse introduced me to the Pamunkey and Mattaponi Rivers, and Don Peterson coached me in the finer points of mountain biking.

And a special thanks to my wife, Lynn, and son, Tom, who accompanied me on most of these trips. We discovered many things about our wonderful state and made many new friends. Lynn still wears a scar on her elbow from a memorable bike trip along the New River; I think she wears it proudly.

Introduction

Virginia is a remarkably diverse state. In writing this book, I fished in the Atlantic surf on a wilderness barrier island, and I fished for trout in a mountain stream. I caught salamanders under rocks on Mount Rogers. I caught clams on the tidal flats of Folly Creek. I rode bikes through railroad tunnels, through wildlife refuges, on mountain trails, and on back roads that lead to Chesapeake Bay beaches. I climbed mountains; I waded in the surf.

In doing this, I discovered the great wealth of wonderful places Virginia has to offer. There have been many guidebooks written about Virginia's natural areas, but I intend this book to do more than explain where to go and what to do. I want it to motivate and entertain, and I believe it will inform. My wish is that you take it with you as you travel the state, and I hope you will learn from it. It would also be very gratifying if you find that you could sit back in the evening with your feet propped up and read a chapter or two and allow me to share with you some of the things I've discovered.

This is not a guidebook in the sense that it is a balanced and objective census of Virginia's natural areas. It's not. It reflects my interests, which include hiking wild places, be they mountain trails or barrier island beaches. I also enjoy bike-riding, fishing, exploring remote waters in small boats, looking at birds, wading streams, and being in places far removed from the traffic and commerce of daily living.

This book also is biased in that I live on Virginia's Eastern Shore and know the area very well. The chapters on the Eastern Shore reflect, I hope, the deep love I have for wilderness beaches, salt marshes, narrow tidal creeks, and the animals and birds that live in these places. These are written, unavoidably, from a resident's point of view. In some other chapters, I'm clearly a visitor, but, I think, a visitor who is certainly enamored.

I'm leery of making lists. The term "fifty outdoor adventures" is not meant to imply that these are the top fifty or the fifty best. I'm sure your list of fifty would be different than mine. Again, it would depend upon your interests, your biases, your choice of a place to call home. This is a personal accounting of fifty wonderful places and activities I've found in Virginia.

My family joined me on most of the trips described here, and I hope this book will encourage readers to explore Virginia as a family adventure. My wife and son and I enjoy many of the same activities, and we find room for compromise in others. Tom, for example, patiently suffers Lynn's and my bird-watching excursions; and we follow him, at a more deliberate pace, on the mountain biking trails. I hope the book will encourage families to be active as a group, to get off the sofa, get outdoors, and enjoy discovering Virginia's natural world together.

Virginia's Wild Side

Virginia

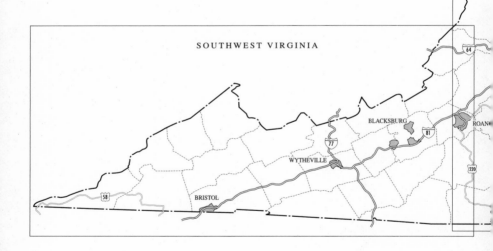

SOUTHWEST VIRGINIA

BLACKSBURG

ROAN

WYTHEVILLE

BRISTOL

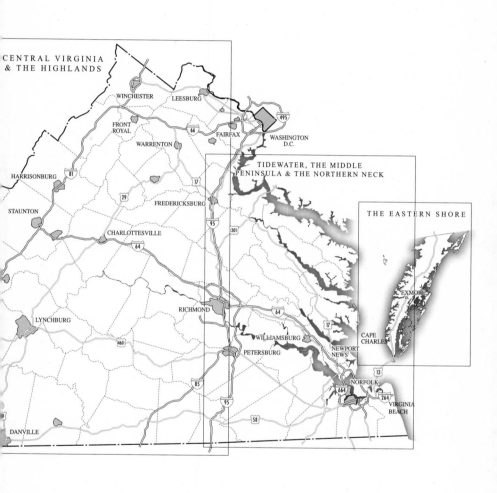

CENTRAL VIRGINIA
& THE HIGHLANDS

WINCHESTER   LEESBURG

FRONT
ROYAL   FAIRFAX

WARRENTON   WASHINGTON
                             D.C.

HARRISONBURG

STAUNTON   TIDEWATER, THE MIDDLE
                             PENINSULA & THE NORTHERN NECK

FREDERICKSBURG

                                        THE EASTERN SHORE

CHARLOTTESVILLE

                             EXMORE

RICHMOND

LYNCHBURG

                    WILLIAMSBURG   CAPE
                                       CHARLES
              PETERSBURG   NEWPORT
                           NEWS

                                       NORFOLK
                                              VIRGINIA
DANVILLE   BEACH

The Eastern Shore

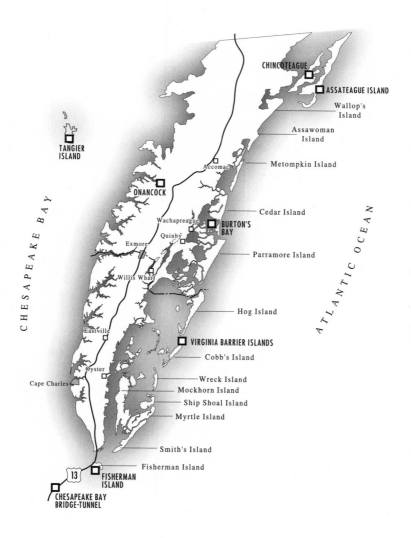

CHESAPEAKE BAY

ATLANTIC OCEAN

CHINCOTEAGUE

ASSATEAGUE ISLAND

Wallop's Island

Assawoman Island

Metompkin Island

Accomac

TANGIER ISLAND

ONANCOCK

Wachapreague

Cedar Island

Quinby

BURTON'S BAY

Exmore

Parramore Island

Willis Wharf

Hog Island

Eastville

VIRGINIA BARRIER ISLANDS

Cobb's Island

Oyster

Wreck Island

Cape Charles

Mockhorn Island

Ship Shoal Island

Myrtle Island

Smith's Island

Fisherman Island

13 FISHERMAN ISLAND

CHESAPEAKE BAY BRIDGE-TUNNEL

On Burton's Bay

Awash in a sea of life

Tom thought he was being attacked by a shark. The water swirled and rose against the bottom of his kayak, and he could feel the pressure beneath him. He stopped paddling and looked into the water but could see nothing. Suddenly there was another swirl, and then it was gone.

"Well, that was interesting," he said.

"I don't see any fins," I said. "You probably interrupted a cownose ray digging clams."

We were in shallow water, less than three feet deep, and a frightened ray would certainly make its presence known beneath a small kayak. "I thought it was going to lift me out of the water," Tom said.

My son, Tom, and I were on Burton's Bay, east of the town of Wachapreague on Virginia's Eastern Shore, exploring this remote area in sea kayaks. An old waterman friend once described Burton's Bay to me thus: "Son, there's a lot of water out there, but it's stretched mighty thin."

Burton's Bay separates the mainland Eastern Shore from the barrier islands of the coast. Cedar Island and its rim of salt marsh run along the eastern side of the bay, and Parramore Island, part of the Nature Conservancy's Virginia Coast Reserve, is visible farther south.

Burton's Bay is perhaps two miles wide and five miles long, but that's just a topo map guess. The perimeter of the bay is like a part of a jigsaw puzzle. There are marshy knobs and indentations that make accurate measurement difficult, and then there are changing salt marshes, tidal flats, and oyster rocks, as well as a four- or five-foot tidal gradient that makes the bay considerably smaller when its waters are "stretched thin."

I've paddled Burton's Bay numerous times, but it wasn't until my recent trip with Tom that I realized I like the bay so much because it is shallow. Those flats and oyster rocks may be a bane to power boaters, but in a kayak, when you don't have to worry about destroying the lower unit in the good old Mercury, you can relax and enjoy life and maybe learn a thing or two.

After Tom's encounter with the "sea monster," I began to watch closely the water around me. Fish were jumping. Little silver mullets were flying through the air like they had been launched by an underwater slingshot. Crabs were finning just under the surface. Quick-moving wakes indicated prey species making a getaway. A single larger swirl suggested that dinner was being served. In the clear, shallow water, plants were growing, and grasses were waltzing in the current.

It struck me that we were in an intensely rich and fecund environment, and part of the reason is that Burton's Bay is so very shallow. Submerged vegetation is lush. Salt marshes are vast and unspoiled, providing nutrients that form the basis of the food chain in this shallow bay. From fiddler crabs to flounder, there is food for all.

Tom and I paddled south along the western edge of the bay. The tide was falling, and we knew of a sandy tidal flat that would be a good turnaround spot and a place to stretch our legs halfway through the trip. Along the way, we skirted the salt marsh, where lush green grasses stood against blue sky. Herons and egrets patrolled the shallow water, searching for small fish.

A kayak is the perfect vehicle for getting close-up views of birds. The southern perimeter of Burton's Bay is lined with tidal flats and oyster rocks, and at low tide these attract hundreds of birds. When we neared an exposed flat, the birds would eye us with curiosity and soon resume their feeding.

On our late-summer trip, shorebirds were migrating through the area, and the summer birds were still around. Whimbrels searched for fiddler crabs on the flats, and skimmers glided alongside our kayaks, their lower mandibles cutting through the still water.

The richness of this seaside environment attracts a wide variety of birds, many of which have adapted special hunting techniques. The skimmer hunts fish as it glides just above the surface of the water. The whimbrel has a large, down-curved bill perfect for probing the burrows of fiddler crabs. Herons and egrets stalk the shallows, then strike with snake-like quickness when prey comes near. Terns and brown pelicans circle over the bay, and when a fish is spotted, they fold their wings and dive at it.

The birds tolerated us well as long as we were on the water, but when we beached the boats on the sandy tidal flat they retreated, and when we stepped out and walked toward them they took flight, calling to each other in alarm.

After nearly two hours in the kayak, it felt good to stretch our legs. The sand was porous and cool after having been inundated at high tide, and the surface of the flat was not flat at all, but scalloped, shaped by the movement of the current.

The sandy flat was soft, and I stepped on something just beneath the surface that was hard, rock-like. I dug under it and pulled out a clam, cherrystone size, perfect for steaming. A dozen of these would be perfect with dinner.

And it occurred to me that this rich natural system, which supports everything from plankton to pelicans, nurtures kayakers as well.

Burton's Bay at a Glance

GETTING THERE

Burton's Bay is north of the town of Wachapreague on the Eastern Shore. Traveling north on U.S. Route 13, turn right onto Route 180 and follow it into town. Wachapreague has a motel, restaurant, and boat-launching facilities. Accomack County maintains a small launching/parking area on the bay itself near the village of Locust-ville at the end of Route 787. The state has a boat-launching facility on Folly Creek, north of Burton's Bay.

FOR FURTHER REFERENCE

The Wachapreague and Accomac quadrangle topo maps show the Burton's Bay, Wachapreague, and Folly Creek areas in detail.

FOR CONVENIENCE AND SAFETY'S SAKE

The bay can become choppy in a breeze. While most of the bay is shallow, a channel runs the length of it, which is part of the Virginia Inside Passage. Most of the tidal flats in the bay are very soft, and footing is not good. The upland surrounding the bay, as well as the oyster rocks, are private property.

Clam Sign

*A quest for clam chowder begins on
the tidal flats of the Eastern Shore*

I stand alone on the tidal flat with
my head bowed, bent slightly at the waist. When I move, I do so with
a shuffling gait . . . slowly, tentatively. If someone were to see me
from a distance, he would think that I am a very old man, perhaps
infirm.

But I am not infirm. What I am is hungry. I am hungry for clam
chowder, and I want it made with salty seaside clams so fresh they
were part of the coastal ecosystem the same day they are eaten.

So I bend at the waist and scour the flat for clam sign, telltale
holes that indicate a clam may be buried beneath the surface. I carry
a clam pick, which is sort of a walking stick with two tines on one
end, and when I spot a suspicious hole I rake the tines around it,
hoping for contact with a clam.

My problem is that many things make holes in tidal flats. Dozens
of species of burrowing worms are out here, and there are shellfish,
crabs, shrimp, and other crustaceans I can't identify. Even birds
make holes in tidal flats. Find a hole with bird tracks around it, and
you probably won't find a clam. The bird was doing its own version
of clamming, with its beak.

But if I find true clam sign, a hole that has a bit of thread-like waste material around it, or a splattering of water, I know I have a candidate for the chowder pot.

Clams live most of their lives buried beneath the surface of the bottom. They exist by sending out two connected siphons, one to suck in nutrient-laden seawater, the other to expel waste. At low tide, when the tidal flat is exposed, these small holes can be seen, thus giving away the clam's location. Clammers call it sign, which is both a noun and a verb; e.g., "The clams are signing good today."

I pull my clam pick across the hole, and it makes a solid, grating sound, not unlike chalk on a blackboard. I work the tines under the clam, rock it free, and add it to the wire basket I carry.

Seaside clams on the seaside Eastern Shore are usually hefty beauties, some nearly the diameter of a softball, and it takes only fifteen or twenty to make a pot of chowder. When the clamming is good, though, I have trouble quitting. We'll have chowder tonight, I reason, and tomorrow night we'll have fritters.

One of the pleasures of clamming is that it is one of the few outdoor sports to have been tread upon lightly by government regulators. There are no seasons, no license requirement for recreational clamming, and the bag limit is a downright generous 250 per person, which translates to a lot of chowder.

Nor is clamming a socially demanding sport. There is no proper clamming attire; I wear hip boots in winter and shorts in summer. You won't find graphite-shafted clamming picks in the Orvis catalog. There are no clamming magazines to subscribe to, no nonprofit organizations whose noble goal it is to save the clam.

All you need to go clamming is a convenient tidal flat in salt water, old sneakers or water shoes to protect the feet, and an instrument to dislodge the clam once you find it. You could dig it out with your fingers or toes, but a large seaside clam is remarkably tenacious and will seldom come willingly to the clam basket. By the time you could gather sufficient clams for the chowder, you would need to make an appointment with a manicurist.

Most sporting goods and hardware stores in coastal communities sell clam picks or clam rakes. A clam rake resembles the garden variety except that it has longer tines, which are handy for prying the clam loose. Rakes are used in shallow water where you can't see the clam holes, or sign, and they can be used on exposed flats when the clams are not signing.

If I'm in a hurry for clam chowder, or on days when I don't have the patience to look for clam sign, I'll take the rake along and simply drag it across the flat, hoping for the familiar scrape of metal against shell. This is clamming at its unsophisticated low mark—sort of like fishing for carp under the railroad bridge compared to casting dry flies for native trout in a mountain stream—but it is effective.

Another favorite clamming method is called treading, a warm-weather sport in that it requires you to get wet. You wade in shallow water, constantly moving your feet in a manner that might be described as doing the old dance step called the twist. Talented treaders can find a clam with their feet and then use the toes to pry the clam loose and lift it to hand level pressed against the opposite leg. Treading should be done where the bottom is relatively soft, making it easy to feel a clam when it is stepped on.

Treading does call for some kind of foot protection. Water shoes are good, as long as the soles are sufficiently thin and pliable that you can feel the clam. Old-time clammers used slippers made of felt.

While clamming is a rewarding sport, the true pleasure comes later, when the time comes to enjoy that pot of chowder. The popular notion is that there are two types of chowder: New England, which is creamy; and Manhattan, which is tomatoey. Traditional Eastern Shore clam chowder is neither. It is a simple mix of potatoes, clams, and clam juice.

My version of clam chowder has evolved over the years, borrowing a bit from recipes for linguine with clam sauce and clam pie. The recipe follows, and now all you have to do is find a friendly tidal flat and go signing.

Folly Creek Clam Chowder

15 to 18 large chowder clams with juice
6 medium potatoes, peeled and cubed

about 1 tablespoon bacon grease
4 to 6 cloves garlic, chopped
1 cup low-fat chicken stock
1 carrot
1 cup Half and Half
ground black pepper to taste
mace
a few sprigs of fresh parsley, chopped

Using a large pan or Dutch oven, saute the cubed potatoes in the
  bacon grease until a glaze forms on the bottom of the pan and the
  potatoes are lightly browned.
Add the garlic and lightly brown it with the potatoes.
De-glaze the pan with clam juice and chicken stock.
Shred the carrot and add to the chowder.
Coarsely chop the clams and add to the pan, along with black pep-
  per, parsley, and a dash of mace.
Let simmer until potatoes are done and chowder has thickened.
Add a cup of Half and Half, stir, and serve.

This recipe yields approximately two quarts of chowder.

Tangier by Bike

*A mountain bike is the perfect vehicle
for exploring this Chesapeake Bay island*

Bike-riding is like religion in that it absolves you of all guilt. I had a friend in college who regularly got wild and crazy on Saturday nights, but on Sunday mornings he was a regular in chapel, a bit bleary-eyed and unsteady but invariably present and repentant.

What brings this to mind is a boat trip my son, Tom, and I recently took to Tangier Island. No, we didn't get wild and crazy. Folks don't do that on Tangier. But we did overindulge. We threw aside all restraint and for an hour or so wallowed in unmitigated gluttony, an act that would bring a black cloud of guilt over the head of anyone remotely interested in his cholesterol level.

If you've ever visited the beautiful island of Tangier and stopped for lunch in Crockett's Chesapeake House, you'll know whereof I speak. Meals here are served family-style, in portions designed for men and women who have been on the bay fishing crab pots since dawn. There are crab cakes, clam fritters, baked ham, homemade rolls, corn pudding, green beans, coleslaw, pickled beets, and pitchers of iced tea, with thick slabs of pound cake for dessert. Other than the crab cakes (two are served), you are welcome to indulge yourself until a black cloud forms over your head.

And now about bike-riding and religion and how both absolve you of guilt. Tom and I went to Tangier aboard the *Captain Eulice,* a former mailboat that sails daily during summer from Onancock. We rode to Onancock on the bikes, rolled our bikes up the gangplank of the *Captain Eulice,* lashed them to an awning post with bungee cords, and sat back to enjoy the hour-and-a-half crossing. Once on the island, we'd have more than an hour to explore the narrow streets by bike, and by then we'd be guiltless gourmands at Crockett's Chesapeake House.

The *Captain Eulice* leaves Onancock at 10:00 A.M., and in summer a soft haze settles over the still water. There are a few homes along Onancock Creek—some new, some dating back to the eighteenth century—but no intense development as seen along so much of our coast.

Rev. Albert Crockett, serving as first mate for the day, pointed out historic sites as we headed toward the mouth of the creek and the open bay. Onancock celebrated its three-hundredth birthday more than twenty years ago, so the town, and the creek that shares its name, has a rich history. Commercial sailing vessels came to the port to load farm produce and to deliver goods from the city. Later, steamboats docked here and ferried passengers and goods to various ports around the bay.

The *Captain Eulice* is the only passenger boat that calls here regularly these days. She's a classic wooden Chesapeake Bay boat, Coast Guard–approved for ninety passengers, who on most days are a mix of Tangier residents visiting friends on the mainland and tourists who have come for a scenic boat ride and a lunch of fresh seafood and garden vegetables.

As the *Captain Eulice* nears the mouth of the creek, the community of East Point appears on the south shore and Ware Point and Sound Beach, a state natural area, on the north. The channel zigzags through a shoal area, and nearly all of the red and green channel markers have active osprey nests atop them.

At the number-one marker we enter the bay, and the still water gives way to a gentle swell, which the *Captain Eulice* cuts through smoothly, showering those in the bow seats with a cooling spray.

Watts Island passes on our right, and soon the water tank and church steeple of Tangier come into view. The port is on the north side of the island, and we slow down and cruise past crab-shedding houses on both sides of the channel. Here, freshly caught crabs are packed for market, some to be served as soft crabs, some as steamed hard crabs, and others shelled out and sold in pound cans of backfin and special crab meat.

When the boat docks, most of the passengers make their way to Crockett's Chesapeake House or one of the other island restaurants for lunch. Tom and I climb aboard our mountain bikes and explore the island streets and pathways.

Tangier is a small island, and you're not going to get an intense workout by pedaling a bike around the town. But a bike is a great way to see Tangier. You can start at the boat dock, ride south along the main street, then cross a bridge and return in a circular route that weaves through residential neighborhoods and crosses a salt marsh.

Intersecting with this main circular route are small roads and paths well worth exploring. One path we took ended at a quiet beach, where children were swimming in the bay.

The reward of exploring the island by bike is that you get to see places that most visitors on foot will miss. And, of course, at the end of the ride, you can park the bikes under the shade tree at Chesapeake House, slake your thirst with a glass of iced tea, and then go after those crab cakes and clam fritters with a clear conscience.

Tangier at a Glance

GETTING THERE

The *Captain Eulice* leaves the Onancock Wharf daily at 10:00 A.M. Memorial Day through October 15. The boat arrives at Tangier around 11:30 and departs at 2:00 P.M., arriving at Onancock at 3:30. There also are daily departures from Reedville and Crisfield, Maryland.

AND WHILE YOU'RE THERE

Spend some time in historic Onancock. There are unique gift shops, antiques stores, and several excellent restaurants and bed-and-breakfast establishments within walking distance of the wharf. Kerr Place, a museum owned by the local historical society, is a short distance up Market Street from the wharf.

Birding on
the Bridge

*The Chesapeake Bay Bridge-Tunnel
is the place to find exotic species*

The waitress gave me a motherly look. "You're not going out looking for birds in weather like this, are you?"

I hated to admit it, but I had already been out on the Chesapeake Bay Bridge-Tunnel for two hours in "weather like this," and it was only the thought of a bowl of hot clam chowder that persuaded me to give the birds a break.

I sipped the chowder, munched a grilled cheese, and kept my eye on the restaurant window in case some interesting birds might appear. My binoculars and notepad occupied the place-setting next to mine, and the chair was filled to the overflow with surplus clothing.

"How did she know I'm a birder?" I wondered.

According to my notes, I had arrived on the Chesapeake Bay Bridge-Tunnel at 9:57 A.M., the temperature was twenty-three degrees, and there was a light wind from the north. It was cloudy and damp, promising snow. For the two previous days the winds had been at gale force from the northwest, and I had been making plans for one of my winter visits to the bridge-tunnel. After the blow, I knew the rock islands that anchor the tunnel tubes would have hundreds of birds around them.

The Chesapeake Bay Bridge-Tunnel, which links the Eastern Shore and Hampton Roads, has in recent years become a favorite winter destination among bird-watchers. It seems an unlikely birding hotspot, this 17.6-mile span of concrete and steel, but the bridge-tunnel makes accessible some prime seabird territory at a time of year when going out in a small boat would be uncomfortable, if not foolhardy.

The bridge-tunnel has long been known as a fishing hot spot, with rock islands and pilings that attract bait fish and crustaceans that game fish prey upon. And the theory holds true with birds as well. Sea ducks by the thousands congregate along the rock islands to dive for fish and shellfish or simply to rest in the shelter of the island.

Four rock islands anchor the ends of the tunnel tubes. Only the southernmost island is normally open to the public, this the location of the fishing pier and restaurant/gift shop. But the bridge-tunnel administration for a number of years has allowed bird-watchers to observe waterfowl on the other three islands. All that's needed is a letter of permission issued for the calendar year. Show this at the tollgate as you pay the fare, and you'll be allowed to stop on all of the islands to watch birds.

I began my most recent island-hopping trip with the northernmost island, since it is closest to my home on the Eastern Shore. My plan was to hit all three of the closed islands and then stop for lunch at the restaurant.

The recent cold front had sent thousands of birds scurrying south. On my first stop, I noted a flock of about seventy-five red-breasted mergansers, a large number of surf scoters, old-squaws, ruddy ducks, and even black ducks, which were something of a surprise on open water.

Great and double-crested cormorants snoozed and preened on the rock island, and purple sandpipers foraged for food on the wet boulders. Five pelicans cruised over, and northern gannets could be seen diving for bait fish in the distance.

Off the southernmost island was a great raft of lesser scaup, the drakes with a dark-blue head, golden eyes, and pale-blue bill (hence the nickname, "bluebill"). I lost count at 250.

The intriguing aspect of birding at the bridge-tunnel is the prospect that you might see a rare species. I met a group from the College of William and Mary who had just spotted a Thayer's gull, a rare winter visitor in the east. Black-tailed gulls, natives of the Orient, have been seen along the span, attracting birders from around the country. The chances of observing rare seabirds are especially good after storms, when birds can be blown inland from their normal haunts far out to sea.

"The rule of thumb is that, the worst the weather gets, the better the birding gets," says Patricia Sumners of the public relations office at the bridge-tunnel. "February is probably the best month because it's cold, windy, and stormy. If you want to see birds, that's the time to go. Just wrap up and get out there."

Sumners says that, as word has spread of the bridge-tunnel as a birding venue, demand has increased for the annual permission letters, and requests are coming from all over the country. "We get close to one thousand requests each year," she said. "People have come from Idaho, Minnesota, and California. We even had a couple from the Netherlands who had heard about the black-tailed gull on a birding hotline and wanted to see it. Serious birders will travel a long distance and go to a lot of trouble to add a bird to their life list."

Interest in the bridge-tunnel as a birding destination is also helping the bottom line, especially in mid-winter when travel is usually at a low mark. "If you multiply each permission letter we issue by the ten-dollar fare, the economic impact is significant," says Sumners. "But most of the people visit several times, and they'll eat at the restaurant and spend some time either on the Eastern Shore or in Virginia Beach, so the total economic benefit to the community is difficult to measure, but it is very substantial."

Bridge-tunnel workers are also getting used to seeing people with binoculars and scopes during the worst winter weather. A few years ago, the few birders who ventured out were indulged, sort of like the harmless-but-eccentric bachelor uncle. Now, birders are part of the winter landscape at the bridge-tunnel, almost a daily occurrence if the weather is sufficiently nasty.

And in the restaurant, the waitresses have come to know us well. We're the ones with the hardy complexions, dressed for the Arctic, carrying binoculars that cost more than the cars we drive. They'll sit us down, give us a nice bowl of soup, and then send us back out in the weather to look for birds.

The Bridge-Tunnel at a Glance

GET PERMISSION
Write to the Chesapeake Bay Bridge and Tunnel District, P.O. Box 111, Cape Charles, VA 23310-0111 for a letter of permission to stop on the man-made islands. The letter is valid for the calendar year.

DRESS WARMLY
It's cold out there. Usually the nastier the weather, the better the birding. You're not far from your vehicle at any time, though, so there are plenty of opportunities to warm up.

AND WHILE YOU'RE THERE
When we make a trip to the bridge-tunnel we usually include additional stops at Fisherman Island and Eastern Shore of Virginia National Wildlife Refuges, which are at the northern terminus of the span. Kiptopeke State Park is just a few miles north of the refuges, and a bird-banding station operates there in the fall. Hiking trails along the bay and a hawk observatory are among the amenities. Campgrounds, a fishing pier and boat-launch facility, and a swimming beach are also available.

Fisherman Island

*Natural history and human history
mingle on this barrier beach*

The bunker looked like a huge
sand dune, and with its shrubby cover of wax myrtle and wild black
cherry, it seemed a natural part of the landscape. But below the dune
lay tons of steel-reinforced concrete, forming rooms and passage-
ways like something from a medieval castle.

Some sixty years ago, men lived here. They slept and ate in the
concrete rooms, and they stood watch atop the dune and from towers, searching the mouth of the Chesapeake for German U-boats
and other vessels that might be entering the bay with malicious
intent.

A group of us recently stood atop the dune on a cold and windy
Saturday, and we scanned the bay, not for an enemy navy, but for
birds and other wildlife. We were on Fisherman Island, whose location at the very tip of the Eastern Shore made it a vital lookout position during two world wars.

But with modern satellite reconnaissance, the lookout posts on
Fisherman are no longer needed. The island has been a national
wildlife refuge since 1973, a temporary home to tens of thousands
of migrating birds and a nesting ground for the largest colonies of
brown pelicans and royal terns in Virginia.

Fisherman Island National Wildlife Refuge (NWR), which is bisected by the Chesapeake Bay Bridge-Tunnel, is closed to everyday visitors, but the refuge staff offers group tours during the fall and winter and on special occasions such as the Birding Festival held each October and the annual International Migratory Bird Celebration each May.

Refuge recreational assistant Nancy Biegel, who led our group, says her office gets many requests for tours in the fall, but few once the weather has turned frigid. But we figured winter would offer several advantages. There would be dabbling ducks in the shallow ponds and marsh creeks, and the diving ducks would be plentiful in the deeper waters. And there would be none of the less desirable critters such as ticks and mosquitoes, which are numerous in warm weather.

So on a winter Saturday we bundled up and met Biegel at the visitor center at neighboring Eastern Shore of Virginia National Wildlife Refuge and drove to a small parking area on Fisherman. The plan was to hike across the island along an old navy road and then to walk along the bay to the point where the bridge crosses the island. We then would hike back along the roadway to the parking area.

It wasn't long before we discovered Fisherman's value to migrating wildfowl. A freshwater pond near the center of the island held dozens of ducks. We counted black ducks, widgeon, gadwall, green-winged teal, wood ducks, hooded mergansers, and pied-bill grebes, all on a pond about the size of a football field. As we hiked through the grass along the pond's edge, a woodcock flushed from the undergrowth.

"We get hundreds of woodcock in the winter," said Biegel. "They migrate southward and gather here on the tip of the Eastern Shore peninsula before crossing the bay. If we get a prolonged freeze, the birds can suffer because they feed by probing into the soft ground for worms and other prey."

The freshwater pond is a magnet for wildlife, according to Biegel, and it adds greatly to the natural diversity of the island. We found numerous animal tracks along the sandy road that runs along the pond. Deer tracks were everywhere, plus those of raccoon, possibly fox, and river otter. One well-worn path led across a set of low dunes, through a greenbrier thicket, and down to the water.

In the sandy road, Biegel picked up a remnant of last summer. A turtle egg, white and leathery, lay exposed. Inside was a tiny but fully formed turtle, long deceased, its head and shell easily defined. An adult turtle had apparently crawled from the pond to the sandy dune, laid a clutch of eggs, and returned to the water. We found other spent shells without occupants, so perhaps some members of that particular turtle generation survived.

Along the road are not only the remnants of nature but those of humans. A jumble of steel and concrete are all that remains of a lookout tower, which was dismantled by Navy SEALS some years ago. A concrete bunker/sand dune looks like great bat habitat, and in a clearing on top of it researchers trap and band hawks during the fall migration. Where the road meets the beach, the remains of a large pier mark the last of the military presence on the island, that of the navy.

"Fisherman Island has had many uses over the years," said Biegel. "It was a quarantine station in the late 1800s and early 1900s when there was a cholera epidemic in Europe. Immigrants would be quarantined here before being taken up the bay to Baltimore. Then it was used for harbor defense during both world wars."

Fisherman Island played a major role in protecting the northern entrance to the bay, with lookout towers, gun emplacements, and bunkers. Sixteen-inch guns were in place on the mainland a mile or so away at what during World War II was Fort John Custis, which later became Cape Charles Air Force Station. The station was turned over to the Department of Interior in 1984 when the Eastern Shore of Virginia NWR was created.

Considering its colorful history, Fisherman is a relatively young island. "A survey in the 1800s showed the island at about 25 acres," said Biegel, "but it has grown to 1,875 acres and is apparently still building."

Some accounts indicate that Fisherman was spawned by a ship-wreck when a vessel carrying linen went ashore on a bar at the tip of the peninsula. The linen was salvaged, but the skeleton of the ship remained on the shoal, and sand began to build around it. The resultant island was named Linen Bar by local residents.

"No one really knows whether that story is true," said Biegel, "but it adds a lot to the colorful past of the region. We do know that the island began as a shoal, or group of shoals, and it's still growing. We can say that about few barrier beaches today."

Fisherman Island at a Glance

GETTING THERE

Fisherman Island National Wildlife Refuge is an island at the tip of the Eastern Shore peninsula. It is closed to everyday visitors, but group tours are offered on Saturdays from October through March and also in May and October for birding festivals. Call the Eastern Shore of Virginia National Wildlife Refuge at 757-331-2760 for information.

AND WHILE YOU'RE IN THE AREA

Eastern Shore of Virginia NWR is adjacent to Fisherman Island and is open daily. A visitor center provides background on the history and natural history of the area, and walking trails provide panoramic views of the tip of the peninsula. Kiptopeke State Park is a few miles north on the Chesapeake Bay and also offers trails as well as camping and fishing facilities.

Beach-Combing

*A walk on the beach brings
tragedy, treasures*

The gull had been a young bird, still in the smoky gray plumage of youth, and it had probably died somewhere off the beach. It bore no markings of a violent death; perhaps it became ensnared in a fishing net and drowned.

When Tom and I came across it, the bird was just beyond the surf zone, delivered there by the last high tide. But we were not the first to find the dead gull. A ghost crab had dug a den beneath the bird and was going about the process of dismantling it, beginning with the most accessible morsels, the eyes and brain. The crab hid in its den as we inspected the bird, no doubt wishing we would leave so he could resume his work.

Surrounding the gull were the tracks of the busy ghost crab, and I could imagine him, once his den was built, circling and inspecting his great find, probing it here and there, not actually settling down to feed yet but prancing about in some sort of ghost crab wonder, thanking whatever crab deity he believed in for his great good luck.

A walk on the beach can bring drama, tragedy, and sometimes treasure. The death of the young gull was a lesson in the capriciousness of life. Its misfortune was the good fortune of the ghost crab, which had done nothing to deserve this windfall, nor was he aware it would be swept away from him by the next tide.

Nature frequently is harsh. A sea turtle lumbers ashore at night and laboriously digs a cavity in the sand in which she deposits dozens of leathery eggs. But predators are at work. A fish crow digs up the turtle eggs as soon as the exhausted mother disappears at dawn into the breakers. A great black-backed gull steals a tern chick. A fox raids a plover nest.

On the beach is the beginning of life; the sea turtles that survive detection eventually hatch and, like miniature versions of their mothers, plod down the berm of the beach toward the sea. The piping plovers that survive the tides, foxes, fish crows, and ghost crabs become adult birds, and in the fall they fly south.

On the beach are other signs of success. The black egg casing of a clearnose skate has washed up. The casing has been split open, and its occupant has long departed, presumably to begin feeding on the small fish and shrimp of the estuary.

We find egg casings of channeled and knobbed whelks; each case, about the size of a quarter, is attached to the other by a stout membrane. Some strings of egg casings may be two feet or more in length, and each translucent compartment holds, or held, dozens of miniature whelks. The casing of the knobbed whelk has a flat edge, while the edge of the channeled whelk casing is sharp. Now and then, if you slice open a casing with a knife, you can find a few tiny whelk shells inside, homes of the few animals that did not make it.

By fall our back porch is filled with treasures from a summer spent beach-combing. We have dozens of keyhole limpets, fascinating little shells in gray or orange that look like miniature volcanoes. We have bits of coral and lacy little stones that actually are colonies of tiny animals called bryozoans, which often build their communities around a pebble or shell. Large clamshells or the shells of sea scallops are put to use in the kitchen as individual serving dishes for deviled crab or clam.

On some warm day in early spring, we'll have a cleaning frenzy and dispose of the shells, the egg cases, the mermaid's purses, and all the other treasures that seemed so collectible when they were picked up on the beach. Then, as winter retreats, we will begin again.

But beach-combing is not strictly a summer sport. Over Tom's Christmas vacation from school, he and I took the little johnboat out to an island on the Eastern Shore. When we pulled the boat into the shallows it crunched through a slurry of ice, but the sandy beach was firm and we walked perhaps a mile, sometimes over shells stacked a foot deep by the currents.

This time we brought home nothing for the back porch collection, knowing that it would soon be replaced. But we saw limpets, moon snails, jingle shells, cockles, arks, clams, scallops, and tiny snails such as wentletraps and ceriths. Jingle shells are our favorite. They are thin, fragile, and nearly transparent, ranging in color from yellow, to orange, to nearly black.

Pick up a few and put them in your pocket and they jingle like loose change. Perhaps not a negotiable treasure, but having them in hand makes me feel somehow richer.

Beach-Combing at a Glance

WHERE TO GO

Virginia has many miles of ocean beach. The resort at Virginia Beach is well worth exploring during the off season. Farther south are Sandbridge, Back Bay, False Cape, and the North Carolina Outer Banks.

EASTERN SHORE BEACHES

Some forty-five thousand acres of barrier islands on the Eastern Shore are owned by the Nature Conservancy and are managed as the Virginia Coast Reserve. Day uses such as beach-combing and photography are allowed on most of the islands, but you need a boat to get to them, and the waters around them can be tricky and dangerous in rough weather. Contact the Virginia Coast Reserve office at 757-442-3049 for information.

ASSATEAGUE ISLAND

Chincoteague National Wildlife Refuge and Assateague National Seashore on Assateague Island provide great opportunities for beach-combing, and you don't need a boat to get there. The refuge and seashore are east of the town of Chincoteague on the Eastern Shore. Phone the refuge at 757-336-6122.

Cold-Weather Canoeing

Winter is a great time to be on the water

Snow had fallen the night before, and it lay on the forest floor like stale icing on a cake. It crunched under my boots with a sugary sound.

The forecast called for sun, but gray clouds were scuttling low over the horizon, promising more snow. A light breeze stirred the pine boughs, and a dusting of last night's flakes fell silently from little drifts caught in the trees.

It was, I figured, a perfect day to go canoeing.

I loaded the little Old Town into the back of the truck and gathered up paddles, life jacket, a dry-bag with a change of clothes, binoculars, lunch, and a bottle of water. I drove down to a friend's farm on Folly Creek, and the field roads were still white and uncut with tire marks. A good sign. I would have the place to myself.

The Old Town canoe is called a Pack. It is only twelve feet long and weighs just thirty-three pounds, but it has a carrying capacity of four hundred pounds. It is a stable and beamy little boat, not designed for long trips but perfect for exploring salt marshes and tidal creeks, which I had in mind.

I hoisted the canoe over my shoulder and carried it down to the creek, then went back for the other things. The water here is very shallow, so I stowed the life jacket under the seat. I lashed the dry bag to the center thwart, figuring that if I did capsize, I'd be able to quickly retrieve my change of clothes, a vital necessity in winter canoeing. Hypothermia is a very real danger, especially when paddling in remote areas such as this.

The tide was rising, about an hour before its crest, and my plan was to paddle with the rising tide to the head of Folly Creek, explore the little feeder streams, and return with the ebbing tide.

The water was flat calm, despite the light breeze, and it moved almost imperceptibly upstream. In the gray light, it looked like sheet metal, a thin layer of dark steel undulating slightly. A brown oak leaf floated past me, providing evidence of the moving current.

I dragged the canoe through a narrow margin of salt marsh, pushed the bow into the water, and then climbed in. I pressed the paddle blade against a tump of grass, shifted my weight forward, pushed, and was soon free of land.

My favorite moments in a canoe are those first minutes on the water, when I rediscover the wonder of balance and buoyancy, rocking side to side slightly to test my limits. On calm days like today, when the water reflects the sky, the feeling is one of weightlessness; the water and the sky are as one, and I am somewhere in between, with only a gentle bow wake to mark where the elements meet.

I usually carry two paddles. For open water I use a lightweight double-bladed kayak paddle. Then, when the creek narrows and begins to meander, I switch to a single-bladed paddle, the better to maneuver the boat.

Folly Creek is a small seaside creek that begins near the town of Accomac and ends at Metompkin Inlet between Cedar and Metompkin Islands, barrier beaches about six or seven miles long. A state boat ramp is on the creek, and it is popular with flounder fishermen in May and June. But I prefer to stay upstream of the boat ramp, away from the people and the traffic.

Much of the wooded land and farm fields near the headwaters are owned by the Nature Conservancy and are part of its Virginia Coast Reserve. Other lands are large family farms, so there is little of the development here that waterfront usually attracts.

What we have is wildlife, and winter is the perfect time to get up close and personal. A bald eagle nests across the creek from where I put in, and great blue herons stalk the shallow waters. Deer can be spotted in the farm fields and along the shoreline, and raccoon tracks are everywhere along the salt marsh.

But winter here is the time for waterfowl, and I saw the first of them as I drove through the woods and down to the point where I launched the canoe. Dapper little buffleheads and hooded mergansers were out in the deeper waters of the creek, diving for small fish.

I could hear the green-winged teal shortly after I launched the boat and began paddling upstream. From a distance, they sound like spring peepers, but it was far too early for peepers, and much too cold.

I knew where they were, but I couldn't see them, even by scanning the salt marsh with the binoculars. A branch of the creek breaks off the main channel and scatters into the marsh and then into the woods. At high tide, the teal would be up in the shallow streams, looking for food and fresh water.

They flushed perhaps a hundred yards from me, and with them were larger ducks, mallards, blacks, and gadwall. But the teal were most numerous; flock after flock of a dozen or more birds, flying quickly and acrobatically across the notch where the marsh enters the woods and then back out to wide water.

I felt bad about interrupting them, but I knew the break in their feeding schedule would be brief. They would move out to another location, resume feeding, and return to this stream later in the day when I had left. Besides, it was good to see them. Although I seldom hunt ducks anymore, one of the rewards of winter here in Tide-water is to share a salt marsh with flocks of wild ducks. It reinforces the fact that there still is some wilderness left among us.

I paddled as far up the stream as I possibly could, until the canoe was brushing cordgrass on both sides. I wedged the boat into some grass near a thicket of wax myrtles, pulled a turkey sandwich from my pocket, and had lunch with a flock of yellow-rumped warblers.

Yellow-rumps are one of the few warbler species that overwinter in Tidewater, and they are plentiful here along these streamside thickets, where they feast on the blue berries of the wax myrtle shrubs. I made a "pissshing" sound, and more yellow-rumps joined the crowd, moving closer to the canoe with obvious curiosity.

By the time I finished my sandwich the yellow-rumps had gotten bored with me, and I with them. A rotting stem of cordgrass was floating downstream; the tide had changed and was now ebbing.

I lay in the bottom of the canoe and stretched, leaning back against the seat. The sun, as predicted, had broken through, and its warmth felt good. I picked up the paddle, reversed to a wide spot, and turned the canoe around and began the return trip.

At the put-in, the sun had melted the little snow drifts from the pine boughs, and the forest floor gleamed in the sunlight. I returned the canoe to the truck and began the trip home, planning to return again soon.

Cold-Weather Canoeing at a Glance

BE SAFE

Take along a change of clothes in a dry-bag, and lash the bag to the canoe in case of a capsize. Tell someone where you're going and what time to expect your return. Take along a cellular phone. Select your canoeing locations carefully and look for sheltered locations protected from wind and wave.

Chincoteague in Winter

Wild birds, wild ponies, and oyster stew

Football fans have their Super Bowl, but I have my own ideas as to what truly can make a bowl super. First, the bowl should be made of thick earthenware to preserve heat, and it should be of generous proportions. Fill that bowl to the rim with piping-hot oyster stew, place it in front of me, and let me have at it.

Super.

The football version of the Super Bowl and my concept of the same have been linked since our family spent a winter living on Chincoteague Island while our home was being renovated. It was then that we began a Super Bowl tradition that lives on today.

Being somewhat contrarian by nature, we have decided not to watch a football game that is endlessly hyped, vastly overrated, and usually about as exciting as soggy cornflakes. Instead, we spend Super Sunday at Chincoteague National Wildlife Refuge on Assateague Island. If the weather is favorable, we take the bikes and explore the twelve miles of road and trail, stopping for lunch on a deserted beach. If the weather is not so balmy, we bundle up and explore the woods and freshwater impoundments and keep a list of the birds we find.

The real pleasure comes at the end of the day, when dusk settles over the island and we retreat to a local restaurant where we order bowls of oyster stew and grilled cheese sandwiches made with rye or pumpernickel bread.

Oyster stew is a wonderfully simple concoction with only three major ingredients: milk or Half and Half, butter, and plump, salty Chincoteague oysters. It's not a dish for the cholesterol-impaired, but after a day of hiking and biking, I convince myself that I've earned it. Chincoteague restaurants serve a nice traditional stew, with fresh oysters cooked just until their edges curl. Gourmet chefs can do many wonderful things with oysters, but let me have them in a simple hot stew after a cold hike, and let them be genuine Chincoteague oysters, with that wild and salty flavor comparable to none other.

My technique for eating oyster stew would make Martha Stewart cringe. First I eat the oysters and most of the stew juice, leaving about a half-inch in the bottom of the bowl. Then the grilled cheese sandwich is torn into bite-size pieces, dabbed in the juice, and thoroughly enjoyed.

Chincoteague is a friendly, family-oriented town with no pretension. You don't have to worry about looking a little trail-weary at the end of the day, and no one is going to give you a second look if you're a stew-dabber.

A number of years ago we spent the winter in a summer rental cottage just off Main Street. The cottage was small, and the plumbing presented certain challenges when the temperature dipped, but we thoroughly enjoyed getting to know the resort island in winter. Indeed, today we spend more time on Chincoteague and neighboring Assateague in fall and winter than in summer, when the island's population of thirty-five hundred can quadruple.

When we lived on Chincoteague, a daily after-work ritual was to take the short drive down Maddox Boulevard and across Assateague Channel to the wildlife refuge, where I would go for a run around the 3.1-mile Wildlife Loop, or, at low tide, on the hard-packed sandy beach.

Like most wildlife refuges created in the 1940s, the mission of the

Chincoteague refuge is to provide habitat for migrating and over-wintering waterfowl. Freshwater impoundments were built, and these attract thousands of ducks, geese, and wading birds. In winter, huge flocks of snow geese constantly trade between the impoundments and mainland farm fields, creating a memorable backdrop for a run or a hike.

While the main constituency of the refuge is wildlife, the numerous trails and roadways provide a great opportunity for outdoor activities for humans. Chincoteague is especially bicycle-friendly, with linked trails that provide a ride of about twelve miles.

A paved bicycle path leads from the town of Chincoteague to the refuge visitor center, which is adjacent to Wildlife Loop. Black Duck Trail links the loop with Woodland Trail, and another trail runs from the loop to the beach.

Most of the trails are paved, although some sections near the beach were washed out during storms last fall and were rebuilt with a clay-and-gravel mix, making these areas more suitable for hybrids or mountain bikes than for narrow-tired road bikes.

The trails are restricted to bicyclists and walkers, although motor vehicles are allowed on Wildlife Loop after 3:00 P.M.

The key to enjoying Chincoteague in winter is the lack of crowds and the abundance of wildlife. The shallow ponds will have snow geese and Canada geese, black ducks, pintails, gadwall, widgeon, teal, and other dabbling ducks. Diving ducks will be seen in the deeper waters of Assateague Channel and Tom's Cove. Offshore, pelagic birds such as northern gannets can be seen diving for fish.

The famous Chincoteague ponies will be wearing their shaggy winter coats this time of year and can be seen anywhere on the refuge, with the overlook on Woodland Trail providing possibly the best view. The ponies, made famous in Marguerite Henry's book, *Misty of Chincoteague,* are rounded up each July; and, after a swim from the refuge to the town of Chincoteague, some colts are sold at auction to raise money for the volunteer fire department.

Deer are plentiful on the refuge as well, especially the sika deer, or oriental elk, a non-native species that was introduced to the island early in the 1900s. Sikas are numerous near the visitor center and often can be seen along the roadside near the refuge headquarters office.

Chincoteague at a Glance

GETTING THERE

The town of Chincoteague is on Chincoteague Island on the Eastern Shore. Take Route 175 east from U.S. Route 13. Assateague Island is a barrier island east of Chincoteague and is home to Chincoteague National Wildlife Refuge and Assateague Island National Seashore. Take Maddox Boulevard east from Chincoteague.

STAYING THERE

While Chincoteague does not have the beach crowds in winter, there still are sufficient visitors to keep most of the major restaurants and motels open. Call the Chincoteague Chamber of Commerce (757-336-6161) for information on accommodations.

BE SURE TO BRING

Plenty of warm clothing. The wind-chill temperature is usually higher on the beach, with a bit of a breeze. Dress in layers; you can always remove an item or two after you've warmed up. Binoculars and field guides are helpful in identifying waterfowl and other birds. A current federal duck stamp, available at wildlife refuges and post offices, will provide you free access to the wildlife refuge.

I Fought the Cobia, and the Cobia Won

*Sometimes the fish is too big
for the boat*

When it comes to fishing, I have low expectations and thus am easily satisfied and not often disappointed. I believe in the first axiom of a fisherman's life: Any day on the boat is better than a day at work. So just by being out there I'm ahead of the game. The fish are simply bonuses that happen to taste good with butter beans and sweet potatoes.

I don't need to catch large and exotic fish to enjoy a day on the water. Our catch is usually representative of a saltwater mixed bag: spot, croaker, a flounder or two, perhaps a gray trout. We'll fish for perhaps two hours, and then Tom is ready to go to the beach.

But sometimes the unexpected happens, calling into question your values and beliefs, rocking the status quo. Recently we went fishing in the Chesapeake Bay, just outside Onancock Creek. We have a fifteen-foot Chincoteague scow, a beautiful little boat, but it's not exactly a dry ride in a chop. It was a bit too chilly to have a saltwater shower, so we stayed close to the mouth of the creek, anchoring in about twelve feet of water just south of the main channel.

We baited up with bloodworms and, predictably, began catching spot, chubby little late-season fish with pale-yellow fins. I had been wanting to try marinating shark and cooking it on the charcoal grill, so I rigged up a 10/0 hook on a wire leader and put on a live spot as bait. I switched on the clicker on the Penn Squidder and put the rod in the rod holder.

After catching a few more spot with the light rod, I had almost forgotten about the live-bait rig, when suddenly the clicker alarm sounded. The line played out, and when I flipped the reel into gear the rod bent dangerously, and whatever was on the other end headed for Hampton Roads.

A big shark, I figured, and probably more than I had bargained for. But as the fish ran it began to surface in a very un-sharklike way, and about fifty yards astern it made a great leap, clearing the water with a crash. I had only a fleeting glimpse of the fish, but three visual impressions registered: dark, big, and forked tail. Huge bluefish? Not likely. But what?

The fish circled and came to the surface again, and I saw the streamlined shape, the dark sides, the broad brownish stripe. A cobia. I had never caught one before.

The fish came toward the boat, saw it, and turned its muscular body downward and disappeared as line played off the reel. It was a big fish and unbelievably strong, not at all like the sharks I had caught before. It didn't jump anymore, and it didn't show again the speed it had used on its first run. It was just strong and determined. If I got it close to the boat, it would turn its body and swim away without a great deal of fuss.

After a while the fish began to tire, and my wife, Lynn, and I realized that the next step in this little drama would be a tricky one. How were we going to get a muscle-bound fifty-pound fish into our little boat, assuming that it would be prudent to do so in the first place?

Lynn cleared out an area in the bow, sent Tom to the stern, and got out the landing net. Our landing net, which is of undetermined age and questionable worth, didn't appear to be much of a match for the cobia. The image of a lion tamer fending off a big cat with a chair came to mind. But it was all we had. After scores of flounder- and spot-fishing trips, the gaff had long since been retired and, as I recall, might have been involved in a yard sale a few years ago.

The cobia had tired to the point where I could lead it in a generally circular pattern, and Lynn was going to try to net it as it came around on the next pass. Perhaps if we both lifted—she with the net and I with the wire leader—we could get the fish over the gunwale. The cobia saw it coming, though, and with a powerful kick threw the net aside and was gone again. The net, which seemed so large and cumbersome when it was in the way in the boat, now appeared woefully small and inadequate.

We made numerous attempts, and each time the fish would simply bull its way out of the net. Finally, on our last attempt, the line parted, the rod went limp, and the fish disappeared into the Chesapeake forever.

I was angry. I was disappointed. I was thrilled. My knees were rubbery. My gosh, what a fish. They say cobia travel in pairs, I told Lynn. We'll go get the other one. I rigged another live bait and put the rod in the holder, then picked up my ultralight and began fishing again for spot and croaker. But it was a half-hearted effort this time. Catching spot and croaker just didn't seem quite as satisfying as it had an hour earlier.

Fly-Fishing in the Chesapeake Bay

Fishing with a fly makes catching croakers a challenge

I recently have taken up fly-fishing, which is a very expensive way of making it more difficult to catch croakers.

If you have fished in the Chesapeake Bay or its tributaries in recent years, you will have noticed that croakers have become the kudzu of fish, covering the bottom of the bay like that infamous green plant covers the roadsides of western Virginia, climbing power lines and felling trees under its very weight.

We went fishing in the Chesapeake recently, anchoring the boat along a narrow channel that runs through a tidal flat at the mouth of Onancock Creek, hoping to catch a speckled trout. We caught croakers. So we moved to the open bay and drifted with the current along the edge of Pocomoke Sound, hoping to catch flounders. We caught croakers. And so we anchored in deeper water, hoping to catch gray trout. We caught croakers.

I have nothing against croakers. They're fun to catch on light tackle, and when they're fried and drizzled with lemon juice, they taste wonderful. Add some fresh corn on the cob, sliced tomatoes and cucumber, and you have a traditional Tidewater summer meal that can't be beat.

(If fried fish teases your cholesterol level upward, try this recipe: Fillet the croakers, cut away the ribs and belly, and spread a little light mayonnaise on the fillets. Then add some Cajun seasoning and broil the fish for ten to 12 minutes.)

The problem is that bottom-fishing for croakers has become too easy; indeed, croakers are making it difficult to catch anything else. There is a story going around that my hometown, Onancock, once an Indian village, got its name from the phrase "O-Na-no-cocker," which in the Powhatan language supposedly means "Oh no, another croaker."

So I bought a fly rod, reasoning that if I'm going to catch croakers, I might as well be a little more sporting about it. Besides, fishing with a fly rod seems infinitely more fashionable than slicing squid and putting it on a two-hook bottom rig. I can now speak the language of nymphs and streamers and debate the merits of weight-forward fly line.

A few years ago our family took a vacation in the Yorkshire Dales in England, staying for a week in a cottage that once was part of a grain mill. A stream ran through the property, and one day two British gentlemen came through fishing for trout. They looked as though they had just stepped out of an ad for Farlows of Pall Mall, the famous fishing outfitter in London.

They wore expensive waders and tweed caps and jackets and colorful neckties. They had wooden creels slung over their shoulders and fancy little cases that held flies. They carried very expensive rods and reels, split bamboo perhaps, and they handled them with grace, launching the fly line in a continuously changing parabola, a ballet along a streambed.

Those two Brits must have been wearing or carrying thousands of dollars worth of trout-fishing gear. I followed them some distance down the stream, which was knee-deep at most, watching them cast. It was a beautiful thing to experience—performance art—but I didn't see them catch any fish.

After watching those gentlemen, the idea of slicing squid and dropping it overboard on a hook seemed, well, a little crude. So I got a nine-foot fly rod with nine-weight, weight-forward, sinking-tip fly line. It set me back close to two hundred dollars even at a closeout sale, but it does make it more difficult to catch croakers.

I tried it out on the flats of Onancock Creek using a streamer I had bought at Farlows in London. I didn't own a fly rod when I bought the streamer, and I didn't buy it because I thought a fish might actually mistake it for food; I simply liked the looks of it.

Amazingly, an American bluefish, either very hungry or none-too-bright, thought the British streamer looked like lunch. The rod bent, the line tightened, and the fish began moving in more directions than a politician at a church social. Like the bluefish, I was hooked on the fly rod.

I have since caught smallmouth bass in the Maury River and rainbow trout at Douthat State Park. My son took some photos when I was fishing the Maury, and as I looked at them the other day I realized that as a fly-fisherman I still am woefully lacking. It was a beautiful section of the stream near Lexington, a picture-postcard kind of place. But I was wearing baggy shorts, a ragged T-shirt, and had mud up to my knees.

I may have been fishing with a fly rod, but I still had my squid wardrobe. I need a colorful tie, a tweed jacket, and sturdy waders. I figure a thousand dollars should cover it. I know it's a lot of money, but not catching croakers is worth it.

Surf-Fishing

On a fall day on a barrier beach,
fish are unnecessary

If you must go fishing and not catch fish, the best place to do so is in the surf of the barrier islands that line Virginia's Eastern Shore.

My wife, Lynn, and I recently took advantage of a spectacular late fall Saturday to go surf-fishing on a barrier beach a few miles from our home. We were hoping to catch a channel bass, or perhaps a black drum, as they migrated south along the coast, but we took chicken breast out of the freezer before leaving, just in case we came home with nothing more than leftover bait and a sunburn.

Surf-fishing is like playing poker. You know you're probably going to leave your money on the table, but you go anyway, because there is a chance of success and because in the past you've been successful just often enough to make you a believer.

Surf-fishing also is an excuse to do something most sane people would not. On a crisp fall day, sweater weather, I took off my shoes, stripped down to my shorts, and waded out, first knee deep, and then after a breaker caught me, waist deep. I stood there for two hours, now and then retreating to the beach for more bait, and watched the surf, felt the pull of the undertow stealing the sand from beneath my feet, and wished to be no place else.

The power of the surf is mesmerizing, especially when you're standing in it, trying to cast a bait far enough beyond the breakers to reach a shallow slough where a channel bass could be foraging. I think of it as high-sensory fishing. The ocean is at first alarmingly cold, and then you become used to it and get comfortable. The sand moves under your feet, you crunch your way through a shell bed. And there is the unending tumble of white water, creating a sound that is loud and constant yet very pleasing and natural.

You don't experience these things when you're bottom-fishing for croakers.

As Lynn and I fished, strings of cormorants made their way along the beach just beyond the surf line. Brown pelicans glided and dove, coming down in a crash we couldn't hear above the surf sound. Behind us, black ducks flew over the salt marsh, searching for shallow ponds and guts in which to feed. They reminded me that our son, Tom, and I need to brush up the duck blind before the season begins.

Lynn and I had the beach to ourselves. As far as we could see, in any direction, there were no other people, only miles of surf, a broad beach, thousands of acres of tidal marsh, and, in the distance, the mainland.

The only immediate evidence of humans was the abandoned Coast Guard station that sits in the marsh on the north end of the island. The station was abandoned in the 1960s and is weathered to various shades of gray. Unlike some beach houses, it is part of the landscape, and has been for years. Between the surf and the old station is a low dune line where goldenrod grows in thick beds in late fall. Both the goldenrod and the station seem to belong here.

Lynn and I shared the beach with several species of gulls, ringbills just moving in for the winter, and laughing gulls in the process of moving to more southerly shores. And there were sanderlings, which would race the waves in and out, foraging amid the froth left by the surf.

Sanderlings are nervous little birds, constantly in motion, as if they had been too long at the coffee bar. Because they burn so many calories, they have to feed constantly. It seems this bird has gotten itself onto a vicious treadmill. It must run in order to feed, and it must feed in order to run.

The beach we were on, like most barrier islands on the Virginia coast, is accessible only by boat, making it sufficiently inaccessible to retain its wilderness flavor. We had launched our little skiff from a public boat ramp nearby and had made our way to the island through several miles of salt marsh channels. We beached the boat; loaded bait, tackle, and lunch into day packs; and hiked across the island to the surf. It's more work than driving your 4x4 to the beach, but the wildness is worth it.

Most of these islands are owned either by the Nature Conservancy, the state, or are protected as federal wildlife refuge. So it's pleasing to know that this coastal wilderness will remain wild, that our grandchildren and their grandchildren will be able to wade in the surf, cast a bait to channel bass, and enjoy the experience so thoroughly they don't need to bring home fish to make the day a success.

Surf-Fishing at a Glance

GETTING THERE

Most of the barrier islands of the Eastern Shore are accessible only by boat, meaning that you need not only a boat, but knowledge of the local waters to reach them. Lacking same, you could book a trip with a local guide. The Nature Conservancy's Virginia Coast Reserve contains about forty-five thousand acres on fourteen islands. Day uses such as fishing and beach-combing are allowed on most of them. For information on permitted uses, write the Virginia Coast Reserve, P.O. Box 158, Nassawadox, VA 23413. Assateague Island east of Chincoteague is accessible by car, and surf-fishing is allowed on this national seashore. The wilderness element, however, is lacking.

FOR MORE INFORMATION

The Eastern Shore of Virginia Tourism Commission can provide information on accommodations, restaurants, and local fishing charters, guide services, and eco-tours. Call them at 757-787-2460, or e-mail them at esvatourism@esva.net.

A Dawn-to-Dusk Search for Birds

The Audubon Christmas Bird Count brings a variety of rewards

I'll have the hot roast beef sandwich on white bread, an order of fries, lots of brown gravy, and a large root beer. And ketchup. Be sure to bring the ketchup.

Now this is comfort food, made even more appetizing by the knowledge that it's well earned. Lynn and I had been out in the fields and marshes since before dawn, looking for birds. We had walked perhaps four miles, sometimes ankle-deep in mud, sometimes tearing our way through greenbrier patches. We deserved to be well fed at lunchtime.

Lynn ordered a big burger with the works, a sandwich you begin eating with your fingers and finish with the knife and fork. She got fries and a soft drink, and the waitress brought us each an unrequested side of homemade cole slaw. We did have that lean and hungry look.

I got out my miniature tape recorder, and Lynn got the census form and a pen. While we waited for our lunch to arrive we began tabulating the results from the morning count. We were participating in the annual Audubon Christmas Bird Count, an event that for more than a century has encouraged amateur birders to get out in the field on a day over the holidays and list all the birds to be found in a specific geographical area.

Lynn and I haven't been participating for quite that long, but we have been counting birds on the same farm for about ten years, long enough to establish a pattern and learn a few things about human impact on the natural world. We do our count on foot, record our sightings on a small recorder, and then transcribe the results on a census form at the end of the day. We begin before dawn and end at dusk.

The farm we count is more than a thousand acres, and it takes us all day to cover the hedgerows, the wooded areas, and the shoreline. By the end of the day we will log seven or eight miles and will end with that wonderful feeling of being very tired but having accomplished something worthwhile.

Our count this year began on an auspicious note. The first bird we saw was a bald eagle, and the third was a peregrine falcon. In between those two came snow geese by the thousands. At dawn they began rising in great flocks from the barrier islands along the coast, flying to mainland farm fields to dine on tender winter wheat. They began flying at first light and continued uninterrupted for about an hour. Counting them was impossible. We entered an estimated figure of five to eight thousand on our census form.

When the sun came up, the wind began to blow, and with the wind went our chances of finding dabbling ducks and wading birds in the shallow waters of Finney Creek, which is the southern boundary of the farm. The wind was howling from the northwest at about thirty; and little Finney Creek, normally a placid stream, had whitecaps.

So Lynn and I began walking the hedgerows—she on one side and I on the other—herding birds along ahead of us. When we reached sunny areas protected from the wind we found the greatest numbers of birds. There were several species of sparrows, wrens, cardinals, titmice, chickadees, towhees, catbirds, mockingbirds, and the ubiquitous yellow-rumped warblers.

In walking the hedgerows, we found our first evidence of how human manipulation of the landscape affects wildlife populations. The farm for years has had many wide, dense hedgerows, which conceal drainage ditches. The farmer this year, though, had cut many of them, mowing the greenbrier and honeysuckle thickets, which have a habit of mooching their way into cropland.

As a result, birds that use this habitat were conspicuously absent from our census. We had only a few song sparrows and white-throated sparrows, which in the past had numbered a hundred or more. We had fewer wrens, no juncos, no quail.

And this was the first year in doing the count that we had no northern harriers or kestrels. The reason was that a large grassy meadow had been cut and disked and was barren ground this year. The small mammals that had used the meadow in the past had gone elsewhere, and so had the birds that feed on them.

But the news was not all bad. We saw two bald eagles, which now are almost commonplace on the Christmas count. The peregrine stayed with us for perhaps an hour, throwing into a panic all the birds around it. And the flights of waterfowl were remarkable. The snow geese numbered in the thousands, and there were higher-than-average numbers of Canada geese, black ducks, and other waterfowl.

For the day, we found forty-nine species of birds, the most numerous by far being the snow goose. I'm not sure whether our day in the field contributes much to scientific inquiry, but Lynn and I find the annual experience rewarding on several levels. Dawn flights of thousands of geese are memorable. And after a long walk, a hot roast beef sandwich goes down deliciously guilt-free.

The Audubon Christmas Bird Count at a Glance

WANT TO COUNT?

Christmas counts are held in many locations throughout Virginia. Contact a local bird club for details, or get a list of count sites by writing to Christmas Bird Count, National Audubon Society, 700 Broadway, New York, NY 10003. Check out the Web site at www.audubon.org.

COUNTING TOOLS

The person in charge of your count circle, the compiler, will give you a checklist of birds you are likely to see. Binoculars and a good field guide are vital for identification. I use a microcassette recorder and dictate count numbers and log them in on the list later. Counting is often a matter of "educated estimates." Just do the best you can. The census list is turned in to the compiler at the end of the day. A five-dollar fee per counter is charged. If you're counting in an area where hunting is allowed, wear blaze orange for safety.

AND IF YOU'RE JUST GETTING STARTED

Volunteer counters reflect a wide variety of skills, from beginner to expert. If you don't feel sufficiently knowledgeable to go on your own, your compiler can probably team you with another individual or group for on-the-job training.

Onancock by Kayak

A day on the water ends with a seafood feast

We were drifting along with a pod of bottle-nosed dolphins, amazed that an animal so large could be so graceful. They arched smoothly out of the water, and in the same movement re-entered with hardly a splash. Indeed, they seemed to move with equal comfort through sea and air, traveling in a group of about a dozen.

We were just off Ware Point on the north side of Onancock Creek on the Eastern Shore, where the shipping channel zigs and zags through sandy shoals as though it had been laid out by an underwater mole with a caffeine overdose. Boat captains have to be on alert when coming and going here; miss one of those red or green navigational aids and you go from a depth of twenty feet to two feet or less, and then comes that sinking feeling of hull plowing sand.

We had little to worry about, though, because we were paddling sea kayaks, trim little sixteen-foot water darts that almost could make way on the morning dew. Your perspective is at just above water level, which makes dolphin-watching especially fun.

Onancock Creek is one of my favorite places to paddle because it presents an unusual combination of history, unspoiled nature, shopping, and wonderful food. In a leisurely day, you can put in at the town harbor, paddle out to Ware Point (where the creek meets the Chesapeake Bay) and back, then finish the trip with a dinner of fresh seafood at one of the outstanding restaurants in town.

The town of Onancock (o-NAN-cock) celebrated its three-hundredth birthday in 1980, so the community has a storied past, most of which is centered around its deep-water port. The Virginia General Assembly in 1680 declared Onancock a port of entry for Accomack County, and approximately fifty acres between two forks of the creek were purchased from Charles Scarburgh, for whom the community was briefly named.

Farmers brought their crops to the Onancock wharf to be sent to market, and they came to Onancock to pick up goods and supplies. First came the sailing ships, and later the steamers, which linked Onancock with Norfolk, Baltimore, and other ports along the bay.

There still is evidence of this history at the Onancock wharf. Hopkins and Bro. General Store was the hub of the shipping business in the nineteenth century, and today is a restaurant and tackle shop. A walk up Market Street will take you to Kerr Place (circa 1797), a former home that now is a museum.

Slip your kayak or canoe into Onancock Creek, and more history unfolds. A short distance out the creek are numerous old homes, some of which were the sites of plantations during the days when Onancock was the port of entry. Finney's Wharf, on the south side of the creek, was another steamboat stop. Across the creek, at Onley Point, is the farm where Virginia governor Henry A. Wise once lived.

At Bailey Point the creek widens and the bay comes into view. Several smaller creeks (Finney's, Parker's) break off from the main channel along the southern shore, and on the north is Parker's Marsh, a vast cordgrass meadow with lots of winding channels that beg exploring. Ware Point on the northern bank and Thicket Point on the south mark the junction of the bay and the creek.

While the creekside farms nearer the town offer reminders of the history of the area, Parker's Marsh is where you want to go to see wildlife and experience the creek as it might have been before Onancock became a port of entry. The shallow tidal waterways have waterfowl in fall and winter, as well as a variety of wading birds such as herons and egrets. Ospreys nest on channel markers, and clapper rails can be heard in the marsh.

It's approximately ten miles round-trip from the Onancock wharf to Ware Point, but, given that most people rarely paddle kayaks and canoes in a straight line, add a few more miles to that and explore some offshoots of Onancock Creek such as Leatherbury Branch, Cedar Creek, and the meandering unnamed waterways of Parker's Marsh.

Onancock Creek is protected by a forested shoreline for much of its distance, so wind is not usually a factor, especially when paddling the upper portions of the creek. The creek widens considerably beyond Bailey Point, however, and at times can be rough, especially if the wind is from the west or southwest.

The creek is relatively shallow outside the marked channel, with depths perhaps from two to six feet. We stay in the shallow water, closer to land, because there's a great deal more wildlife to see in this edge where land meets water, and we prefer to avoid motorboat traffic. Being in a channel in a small boat, with a large powerboat bearing down on you, can definitely give you the feeling of being a target.

A paddling trip on Onancock Creek can't be complete without also taking a walking tour of the town. In addition to Hopkins Store and Kerr Place, there are art galleries, antiques and gift shops, and probably more restaurants per capita than any town in Virginia. Some offer family fare and deli-style offerings, while others feature local seafood and other specialties prepared and presented with an artistic touch.

And somehow that makes kayaking Onancock Creek even more pleasurable, knowing that your reward might soon be some fresh seafood taken from these very waters.

Onancock at a Glance

GETTING THERE

From U.S. Route 13 on the Eastern Shore, turn west onto Route 179 in Onley. The road terminates at the Onancock Wharf.

STAYING THERE

There are numerous motels and inns in the Onley and Onancock area. Onancock also has several bed-and-breakfast establishments. Contact the Eastern Shore Chamber of Commerce at 757-787-2460 for information. Or enter the words "Onancock, Virginia" into your favorite Internet search engine.

BE SURE TO BRING

If you plan to kayak the entire ten-plus-mile length of the creek, a sea kayak in the sixteen- or seventeen-foot range would be a good choice. Shorter boats are nice for exploring narrow and winding creeks because they are maneuverable, but on longer trips they can be tiring. If you don't have a kayak, Hopkins and Bro. Store offers rentals. The Pungoteague Quadrangle topo map (scale 1:24,000) covers the entire creek and is a good reference.

FOR SAFETY'S SAKE

Bring appropriate safety gear, such as life jacket and bilge pump. When paddling, stay out of the marked channel. Onancock Creek is relatively rural, but there can be substantial boat traffic on weekends, and low-slung kayaks are not highly visible on the water. Bring sunscreen, insect repellent, a cell phone, drinks, snacks. Check the weather forecast before you set out.

Wood Aerobics

Get a great workout and save on the heating bill

For some time now I've been participating in a workout plan that combines cardiovascular conditioning with strength and coordination training. The great thing about it is that I don't have to pay gym fees or club memberships, nor do I have to follow expensive diet plans. Fact is, my workout plan is making me money by trimming my heating bill a few hundred dollars a year.

I call the plan wood aerobics. All I need for an invigorating workout are my old pickup truck, the chainsaw, a splitting maul, and safety equipment such as eyeglasses and ear protectors (say what?).

My grandfather had a similar workout routine, but his pickup truck was mule-powered, and he alone provided the power for the power saw. I don't think he had a catchy name for his workout, at least not one that could be used when the kids were around.

It did work, though. He was a sinewy old dude. "Buff," grandma might have said.

When we renovated our house a few years ago, we put in a heat pump system, which is wonderful, but I missed a concentrated source of radiant heat. Somehow it just didn't feel right, spending a winter morning out in the marsh, then coming in for a cup of hot chocolate and warming my behind over the floor vent.

I wanted a source of heat that would scorch your underwear if you got too close. I wanted a source of heat that you could place a pot of clam chowder on and let it simmer lightly all day, filling the house with an incredible salty and sweet aroma, making everyone impatient for dinner.

So we bought a wood stove, actually a fireplace insert, and put it in the basement where I work, so I can undergo clam aroma-therapy all day and periodically take breaks to rustle the coals and test the chowder. A spoon hangs from the fireplace mantel.

At about the same time, we sold some timber on a small farm the family owns. When the foresters cut the pines, we asked them to stack some hardwoods at the edge of the field road. And so began my wood aerobics workout routine, which goes like this:

Warm-up: I drive the pickup truck to the farm, walk down to see if there are any ducks on the pond, then select the proper music on the truck radio and crank up the volume. My musical selection can be anything from classical to classic rock. Beethoven's Ninth is good wood aerobics music. So are the Stones. Barry Manilow isn't.

I then prepare lunch. I pop the hood and put a meatloaf sandwich wrapped in foil on top of the exhaust manifold. By noon it will be heated through.

Cardio: I tie a rope to a log and to the truck bumper and pull the log free of the others. I then crank up the saw and cut the log into sections about eighteen inches long. This is the easy part.

Intense cardio: I stand the small logs on end, top side up for easier splitting, and then I go to work with the splitting maul. On a good day, I can split a log with one shot. More likely, it takes several, especially if the log has knots, joints, or twisted fibers that defy metal. Helpful hint: Don't aim at the top of the log you're splitting, aim at the bottom. Think through it. That's where you want the maul to go. Visualize.

Strength and coordination: Once the logs are split, the firewood is loaded into the truck. Lift, carry, stack. Lift, carry, stack. I do numerous reps, numerous sets. That's what strength training is all about. Osteoporosis is not going to get me.

Cool down: Remember the meat loaf sandwich? It's ready, and a root beer is in the basket with the chainsaw oil. Foil packets of ketchup are in the glove compartment. I stretch out behind the wheel, noting that the truck is considerably lower than it used to be. I adjust the rearview mirror. The meatloaf is thick and warm, a sinful reward. Ketchup oozes out between bites.

And so goes the wood aerobics workout. The final step, unloading and stacking the wood at home, is a calming postlude, done slowly and with satisfaction as the woodpile grows.

I perhaps have been selfish over the years in keeping the wood aerobics workout to myself. The fitting thing would be to share.

Producing a video seems somehow presumptuous and mercenary. I should just get a few workout buddies together and go down to the farm. I'd coach them through the warm up, the cardio, and the strength sessions. Then they could come over to the house and unload the wood and stack it along the fence at the rear of the garden.

I'm sure they would agree that it's a fine workout, providing both aerobic conditioning and resistance training. It's the kind of thing personal trainers get the big bucks for. But me, I'd do it for free.

Tidewater, the Middle Peninsula, and the Northern Neck

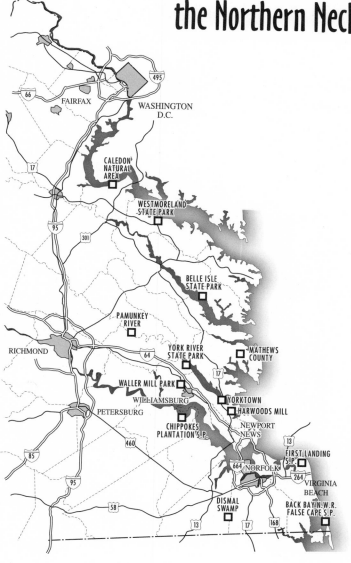

495

66 FAIRFAX

WASHINGTON D.C.

17

CALEDON NATURAL AREA

WESTMORELAND STATE PARK

95

301

BELLE ISLE STATE PARK

PAMUNKEY RIVER

RICHMOND

64

YORK RIVER STATE PARK

MATHEWS COUNTY

17

WALLER MILL PARK

WILLIAMSBURG

PETERSBURG

YORKTOWN

HARWOODS MILL

CHIPPOKES PLANTATION S.P.

NEWPORT NEWS

460

13

85

FIRST LANDING S.P.

95

664 NORFOLK

264

VIRGINIA BEACH

58

DISMAL SWAMP

BACK BAY N.W.R. FALSE CAPE S.P.

13

17

168

King William on the Grill

The croaker is a fine game fish in need of a publicity agent

Back in the days when gray trout were measured in pounds instead of inches, I grew to dislike croakers. To be more accurate, I was aggravated and inconvenienced by croakers, which insisted upon taking my bait before it got within range of the more desirable gray trout, which would weigh six pounds or better and would take line from my little spinning reel in a long, screaming sizzle.

Sometimes I would catch two croakers at a time, leaving no bait at all for the trout. I would hoist them over the gunwale as they snorted and flipped, and I'd de-hook them and toss them into the cooler and take them home and fillet them for the neighbors.

If I caught nothing but croakers, I'd pull anchor and move to another location, hoping to avoid them and attract the trout. Croakers were like little sisters who wouldn't go away when you were trying to impress the head cheerleader.

Now that I'm a bit more mature, and now that a sixteen-inch trout is considered a large fish, I'm much more kindly disposed toward croakers. In fact, the croakers I've been catching recently have been bigger than the trout I've been catching, and when I baste them with butter and cook them on the charcoal grill, they taste very, very good.

I'd never have admitted this during the days when gray trout regularly went five pounds or better, but I now go fishing for croakers. We had company last weekend, and I went out Saturday morning to catch some fish for Saturday dinner. I had croakers on my mind, and my thoughts were of boneless little fillets, dabbed with mayonnaise, sprinkled with Cajun seasoning, and broiled until just done.

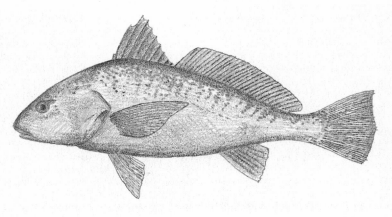

Like thousands of people who live anywhere near salt water, I've come to enjoy fishing for croakers. After all, the fish can be found nearly anywhere: among the navy ships of Hampton Roads, in the lower James, York, and Rappahannock Rivers, on both sides of the Eastern Shore peninsula, and nearly anywhere in the Chesapeake Bay. Striped bass may be the glamour fish of the Chesapeake, but ask the charter skippers in the Middle Peninsula and Northern Neck, and they'll tell you most of their customers visit with the idea of taking home croakers.

The croaker won't take your bait and head for the next area code like a big trout, and it won't put on an aerial show like a bluefish, but on light tackle a croaker will give a good account of himself, especially during those first few seconds when you say, "Get the net, Roy, I've got a big one this time."

When our son, Tom, was small, he developed a special affinity for the croaker, a fish that provides instant gratification. He caught his first while standing in the bottom of the boat with the aid of a walker. He must have been less than two. We had a croaker ritual that went on for several years. We would anchor the boat, get Tom baited up, and he would have a fish on before my wife and I could get our terminal tackle wet. "I caught the first fi-iish," he would chant.

Croaker populations are cyclical, and after dropping off in the 1980s the fish have been making a comeback over the past few years. Despite my earlier unenlightened attitude, I'm glad to see them back.

The croaker still is not appreciated in all quarters, however, and I think part of the problem is the fish's name. "Croaker" simply does-n't have a romantic, adventurous ring to it, although the name does accurately describe the sound the fish makes as it comes on board.

According to a brochure published by the Virginia Institute of Marine Science, the scientific name of the croaker is *Micropogon undulatus.* I have no idea what this means, but the brochure goes on to explain that the fish was known in the 1800s as the King William, which certainly evokes a loftier image than "croaker" or "hardhead," another well-used colloquial name.

Perhaps we should restore the croaker's noble old title. "Get the net, Roy, I think I've got a King William on," might soon be heard throughout the bay, instead of "Geez, another croaker."

In politics, they call it spin doctoring, and it is widely practiced during presidential debates. It means, simply, to make something appear much better than anyone thought it appeared.

To you and me, mud is mud. But given the proper spin, mud becomes a nutrient-rich soup of organic life that supports an entire estuarine food chain. Much of the spin doctored in politics deals with mud, and with the digestive remains of adult male bovine mammals.

But we digress.

Croakers have suffered from an image problem for years, and it's time to put an end to it, whether that means going back to the noble name of King William or coming up with something more exotic and adventurous, like wahoo, or tarpon, or cobia. Is there a spin doctor in the house?

If, as I did for many years, you continue to question the value of croakers, try this. Marinate a few good-sized ones in lemon juice and teriyaki sauce for a few hours. Lightly coat them with butter or margarine to prevent sticking, and put them in one of those wire grates designed for cooking fish on a charcoal grill.

Get the coals good and hot, melt some butter and add lemon juice and teriyaki, a little pepper, Old Bay, and stir. Put the fish on the grill, baste them regularly, and cook until they are just done.

Slice a few fresh tomatoes, put on a few ears of sweet corn, and call the neighbors. Tell them to come on over. You have King William on the grill.

Catching Croakers at a Glance

BEST BAITS
Croakers will take a lure, but they prefer baits such as strips of squid, peeler crab, or bloodworm. Live minnows will also attract them.

BEST TACKLE
Light tackle makes croaker fishing challenging. A light spinning rig with six- to eight-pound test line is perfect. Or try a fly rod on shallow flats. Anchor along the edge of a dropoff, and fish on the bottom using a standard two-hook top-and-bottom rig with just enough weight to keep the bait on the bottom. Croakers are bottom feeders and have small mouths, so use small hooks.

WHERE TO FISH
Croakers can be found most anywhere in the Chesapeake Bay area. Charters operate out of many towns on the bay, and headboats can get you out to where the croakers are at a very reasonable price. Check with local tourism offices for information. And don't overlook fishing piers. Croakers can be caught very close to shore, and a day of pier fishing usually means an evening of fine dining.

Birding by Bike

*Riding the trails at
First Landing State Park*

Most bird-watchers are the slow and silent types. They prowl through the undergrowth as stealthily as Indian scouts in old Western movies, binoculars drawn, field guide at the ready.

I like to go birding at ten miles per hour. That's my average speed when riding my bike from the Trail Center at First Landing State Park out to the Narrows and back. It's a round trip of about twelve miles, and it takes me about two hours, including time for a sandwich break on the park benches next to the boat ramp.

I'm not exactly silent, either. My old mountain bike tends to rattle over the exposed roots of Cape Henry Trail, and I've tied a sleigh bell to my bike bag, which makes me sound like Christmas in August when I come pumping up the hill.

I'm not trying to be loud and obnoxious; it's just that I realize how aggravating it can be when a cyclist approaches a pedestrian and the pedestrian is unaware of his presence. So the bell, which is an actual antique and is very melodic, let's folks know I'm coming should I forget to say something like, "Passing on your left."

Birding by bike is a great sport, providing a good cardiovascular workout with an opportunity to get out and enjoy nature. You won't see prothonotary warblers while pedaling the stationary bike at the gym.

First Landing State Park is one of the best places I know of to combine a bike ride with a little wildlife observation. The bike trail runs through a heavily forested area for three miles—Spanish moss dripping from the trees—and then it crosses Sixty-fourth Street and runs along an old dune line for nearly three more miles to the Narrows, where there's a small beach and boat-launch area.

Along the way, you'll pass through bald cypress swamps, forested upland, and shrub thickets, and you'll cross a wooden bridge spanning a salt marsh. You're likely to see anything from prothonotary warblers, which nest in the cypress swamp, to ospreys, which build huge nests in pine snags in the salt marsh area.

Admittedly, bird-watching is by tradition a contemplative sport, one most successfully done with a certain languor, but I find that, if I keep my eye out for birds while biking, it makes the ride all the more fun. I ride for exercise, but that doesn't mean it has to be all sweat and drudgery.

Luckily, Virginia Beach has First Landing State Park, an oasis of green in a sprawling resort city, where there is an opportunity to combine an outdoor workout with some nature observation. Thousands of tourists come to the city each week, many of them zipping through the park on Shore Drive without realizing what a jewel we have here.

First Landing has nineteen miles of trails, most of which are designated hiking trails. Bikes are allowed only on Cape Henry Trail, which is just under six miles long. Most of the walking trails run along old dune lines, which are sandy and fragile, thus the bike ban. But Cape Henry Trail will give riders a chance to combine exercise with a little wildlife watching.

The trail begins at the parking area off Shore Drive. Trails are color-coded and well marked, and Cape Henry Trail is wide enough here for cyclists to pass each other, and pedestrians, without fear of a mishap. The trail is flat, relatively straight, and made of hard-packed clay and gravel. Exposed tree roots and wet-weather puddles make it more suitable to off-road bikes rather than street bicycles.

Once Cape Henry Trail crosses Sixty-fourth Street, it changes character a bit. It crosses a cypress swamp via a wooden bridge, then becomes narrow and twisting as it threads its way along an old dune line. It is by no means a mountain bike trail—there are no obstacles or steep climbs and drops—but exposed roots and soft sand make you pay attention. The trail is not single-track, so care should be taken when meeting other riders or pedestrians.

While Cape Henry Trail is the main drag of the park, other footpaths that connect with it are well worth exploring. Park the bike and hike Osmanthus Trail, a three-mile circuit that offers peace and quiet in a lowland forest. Bald Cypress Trail, just behind the Trail Center, provides boardwalks and observation decks over cypress swamp habitat, and it crosses forested dunes. This is a 1.5-mile self-guided interpretive trail, and a very informative guide is available for a small fee at the Trail Center.

First Landing, like most state parks, has a diverse constituency. Some come for exercise; it's a safe place to go jogging or cycling or take the dog for a walk. Others enjoy watching wildlife in a habitat that remains rich and diverse, despite the nearness of civilization. And for some of us, First Landing provides all the above.

First Landing at a Glance

GETTING THERE

First Landing State Park, formerly known as Seashore State Park, parallels Shore Drive and Atlantic Avenue in Virginia Beach. The main access point is at 2500 Shore Drive. Newly renovated contact stations are on the beach side of Shore Drive as well as at the trail area. A modest parking fee is charged. Campsites and cabins are available. Call 757-481-2131 for information.

BIKING IN THE PARK

Bicycles are allowed only on Cape Henry Trail, a six-mile dirt track running from the Trail Center to the Narrows. Pedestrians use the trail quite heavily, so riders should be courteous when meeting or overtaking walkers or slower riders. Slow down and let your presence be known.

WILDLIFE WATCHING

The diversity of habitat makes the park a magnet for a wide variety of wildlife. Cypress forests will have warblers and other migratory birds in spring and fall. Ospreys and other birds of prey can be seen in the open areas of salt marsh. Bald Cypress Nature Trail, located just behind the Trail Center, provides a good introduction to the wildlife and plants of the park. Be sure to stop by the center and pick up a trail guide before you set out.

Back Bay and False Cape

*A refuge and a state park
provide a taste of wilderness*

The otter clearly wasn't expecting company, and it snorted in disgust when we surprised it on our bikes. We were riding along the dike roads at Back Bay National Wildlife Refuge, and the otter had just emerged from the woods and was headed for an impoundment, no doubt on some urgent otter business.

We stopped the bikes and watched it; it was sleek and black, with hair slicked down like a fifties rock star. It turned and regarded us with more curiosity than fear, then it glided down the bank and swam into a marshy thicket, where it probably watched us until we left.

There's no telling what you're going to come across on these dirt roads at the Back Bay refuge and neighboring False Cape State Park. Otters are a regular part of the mix, as are feral hogs, horses, deer, and the occasional reptile. The shallow ponds might have ducks and geese, wading birds, and migrating shorebirds. Ospreys fly overhead, and the pine woods and myrtle thickets are usually full of songbirds, especially during the spring and fall migrations.

For an area as populated as Virginia Beach, Back Bay and False Cape offer a welcome respite, a chance to escape the traffic and strip malls and enjoy the quiet of nature. The refuge and state park are only a few miles south of the resort strip, but, in character, they are in different worlds. Sometimes, on weekdays, you can ride the trails and have the place to yourself.

Back Bay refuge begins just south of the community of Sandbridge and includes eight thousand acres of ocean beach, marsh, forest, and farmland. False Cape adjoins the refuge and extends southward some six miles to the North Carolina line. The refuge and state park include about ten miles of undeveloped ocean beach.

False Cape, despite its nearness to a major population center, may be Virginia's most remote state park. It is accessible only by walking or bicycling the dike roads at Back Bay refuge, walking the beach, or taking a boat. And in winter, when the dike roads are closed to the public, your options are reduced even further. (Group visits aboard a tram are offered during the winter.)

But the park's remoteness and the refuge's emphasis on wildlife are what make this area so special and such a contrast to the more-populated beach community a few miles to the north.

The refuge was created in 1938, and, like many coastal refuges built during that period, its mission was to provide a sanctuary for migrating waterfowl. That mission has not changed, although the natural life at Back Bay certainly includes much more than ducks and geese. The dike roads are closed to the public from November through March to help provide a safe haven for waterfowl, and the four miles of ocean beach are limited to nature study and fishing. Swimming, surfing, and sunbathing are not allowed.

Although Back Bay's main constituency is wildlife, from April through October it is an ideal place for a bike ride, especially if your idea of a good ride includes an up-close look at wildlife and zero encounters with internal combustion engines.

Tom and I rode the Back Bay dike roads and the trails at False Cape recently, clocking about eighteen miles on our bike odometers. We began at the visitor contact station at the end of Sandpiper Road and headed south along the marked trail. The refuge alternates bike access on dike roads according to the season, and when we visited the western roads were open, offering a nice view of Back Bay as well as the shallow impoundments.

Later in the year this route will be closed, and the eastern road behind the dune line will be opened. Our preference is the western route because it crosses a wide variety of habitats and thus provides access to more natural diversity. The road behind the dunes is a three-mile straight stretch that can make the return ride a bit tedious if the wind is from the north and you've already ridden fifteen miles on dirt.

The dike road joins False Cape State Park just over three miles south of the visitor contact station. A large shallow pond with an elevated overlook is on the left as you enter the park, and a small office and contact station are about one mile inside the park. At the contact station, a right turn will take you to the Barbour Hill boat landing, or you can turn left and head farther south.

Tom and I headed south, deciding to ride to the Wash Woods Environmental Education Center to have our lunch. The trail here is wooded and winding, with large pines and live oaks. We could see where feral hogs had been rooting in the understory, and tracks of wild ponies pockmarked the sand alongside the trail. We could hear the trill of prairie and pine warblers in the forest canopy.

The environmental education center was the halfway point of our ride and the perfect place to break for lunch. The center is a former hunt club, with an expansive view of Back Bay and Cedar and Little Cedar Islands. The facility is now used to accommodate groups studying the natural history of the area. Tom and I unpacked our sandwiches and made use of the picnic tables as we watched ospreys fish the shallow waters of the bay.

After lunch, we visited the remnants of the community of Wash Woods, just east of the environmental education center. Wash Woods is said to have been founded by survivors of a shipwreck, and it eventually grew into a sizable community, until a rising sea level encouraged residents to move to the mainland. All that remains today is a small cemetery and the foundation and steeple of the village church.

A sandy trail leads from the cemetery across the dune line to the ocean, and Tom and I parked our bikes and walked the half-mile to the beach, which was deserted. In the distance, we could see the skyline of Virginia Beach, hanging ghost-like over the horizon. As the crow flies, it was a matter of only a few miles. But it was a world away.

Back Bay and False Cape at a Glance

BACK BAY NATIONAL WILDLIFE REFUGE

The refuge entrance is at the end of Sandpiper Road south of Sandbridge. An entry fee is required. Dike roads are open to bicyclists and walkers from April through October, and there is an interpretive center and walking trail near the visitor contact station. The refuge offers numerous public education programs. Phone 757-721-2412 for information.

FALSE CAPE STATE PARK

The park offers primitive camping, and groups can be accommodated at the Wash Woods Environmental Education Center. Interpretive programs, hikes, and canoe trips are available. Phone 757-426-7128 for information.

IF YOU RIDE

The dike roads and trails are mostly hard-packed clay and gravel, and portions of the False Cape trail have soft sand. The riding is easy, but a mountain bike with wide tires would be preferable to a road bike. There are few facilities, but soft-drink machines are available at the state park office and at the environmental education center. Bring your lunch or snack.

The Great Dismal Swamp

A natural treasure, with a bit of a reputation

Tom and I had just put up our tent when the lock-keeper came over and shared some unwanted information with us. "Yesterday I killed a rattlesnake big around as my arm right where you pitched your tent."

I guess that's one snake we won't have to worry about.

We had parked our truck at the boat landing on U.S. Route 17, launched our canoe, and paddled up the Feeder Ditch to the Army Corps of Engineers dam near Lake Drummond in the Great Dismal Swamp. The corps maintains a campsite here, nothing fancy, but a place where you can pitch your tent, cook a steak on a charcoal grill, and have a leisurely dinner on a picnic table in a screen house. That's what Tom and I intended to do.

Tom was sixteen at the time and had been reading about the Dismal Swamp in school but had never been there, other than zipping through the periphery on Route 17 on our way to North Carolina. So we loaded the old F-150 with camping stuff, lashed the canoe to the top of the truck, kissed his mom goodbye, and set off for a Dismal Swamp adventure.

When I was Tom's age, I read about the Dismal Swamp in a thick, blue textbook on Virginia history. George Washington, when he was

young and idealistic, tried to drain it. Col. William Byrd surveyed
the state line through it and was not impressed. "Foul damps ascend
without ceasing and corrupt the air," he wrote.

William Drummond, the first colonial governor of North Carolina, discovered the lake in the center of the swamp while on a
hunting expedition that, for reasons unknown, he alone survived.
Drummond was later hanged, drawn, and quartered after being
charged with treason.

So the Dismal Swamp comes with its share of baggage, and I'm
not sure that history textbooks even today dare suggest that what we
have here is a diverse and valuable ecosystem with a wealth of animal and plant life. Like the lock-keeper who warned us of rattle-
snakes, there is the persistent and perhaps pleasurable notion that
danger lurks here. Our culture has been taught to beware of swamps.
Indeed, the term Dismal Swamp could be considered a redundancy.

Many writers over the years have visited the swamp and tried
valiantly to convince their readers that nothing is dismal about the
Dismal, but few have enjoyed unqualified success. One of the most
entertaining attempts was made by John Boyle O'Reilly, an Irish-

man, whose book, *Athletics and Manly Sport,* describes a canoe trip to the Dismal in May 1888.

O'Reilly and a friend paddled two cedar canoes from Norfolk down the Dismal Swamp Canal to Lake Drummond. "There is no other sheet of water like this anywhere," wrote O'Reilly. "No other so far removed from the turbulence of life, so defamed, while so beautiful."

While O'Reilly was taken with the beauty of Lake Drummond and impressed by the variety of birds he saw, he, too, became a victim of reptile phobia. He wrote that while paddling the canoe he kept his pistol handy, firing now and then into the cane thickets to deter any cottonmouths that might entertain thoughts of attacking.

O'Reilly and his friend escaped the fangs of cottonmouths, but they apparently fell victim to the barbs of some local pranksters, who convinced them that the cottonmouth was harmless compared to the deadly green snake. "The most deadly snake in the swamp is one of the smallest," wrote O'Reilly. "He is about 12 inches in length, green in color, like that of the poplar tree in which he lives. We escaped him most fortunately, for before we heard of him we had deflowered many poplars of their beautiful blossoms."

I wondered, after reading O'Reilly, whether some of the great-grandchildren of those local pranksters might have grown up to be Army Corps lock-keepers.

Tom and I saw no snakes, which was something of a letdown, like going to a hockey game and not having a fight break out. We beached our canoe at the campsite, put up our tent, unloaded our supplies, and then portaged about fifty feet around the dam and paddled out to explore Lake Drummond.

Like O'Reilly, we were impressed by the quiet. We paddled south along the edge of the lake and listened. In the distance was the staccato rattle of a downy woodpecker, then came the more rhythmic chopping of a pileated. We flushed a pair of wood ducks from behind a cypress stump, and a kingfisher flew off ahead of us.

Lake Drummond is now part of Great Dismal Swamp National Wildlife Refuge, a 110,000-acre sanctuary created to protect the diverse animal and plant life that exist here. The Dismal Swamp is said to be the nesting site for seventy-five species of birds, and is the temporary home for many more migrants that pass through in spring and fall. It is the northernmost of a series of southern coastal swamps, and so is the northern territorial limit of many animal and plant species, such as the dwarf trillium and wild camellia.

The great value of the Dismal is that it is a truly wild thing, a place that is dangerously close to millions of people, yet seemingly untouched. And the swamp's storied past contributes to the experience of going there. It is like Hemingway's big two-hearted river: part of it is beauty and light, and part is forbidding and dark.

Dismal Swamp at a Glance

GETTING THERE
A boat launch facility is on U.S. Route 17 in Chesapeake about six miles north of the state line. From here, take the Dismal Swamp Canal south for about a quarter of a mile. The Feeder Ditch will be on the right. It's a paddle of about three miles to Lake Drummond.

STAYING THERE
Camping is allowed at the Army Corps of Engineers dam site. There are screen houses, grills, and picnic benches; and running water is available during warm months. There is no charge for camping.

THE WILDLIFE REFUGE
If you don't want to take a boat to Lake Drummond, the best way to see the refuge is to enter on the Suffolk side on White Marsh Road. Washington Ditch Road and Jericho Lane both intersect White Marsh Road south of Suffolk. Lake Drummond is 4.5 miles down Washington Ditch Road, which parallels a canal dug many years ago to drain the swamp. This road intersects with others that crisscross the swamp and offers good off-road biking. Phone the refuge at 757-986-3705 for more information. Visit the Web site at http://greatdismalswamp.fws.gov.

Alive in the Killing Fields

A sixteen-mile ride at Yorktown
Battlefield brings history to life

There is blood on the ground here.

Where we stand, on a siege line at Yorktown Battlefield, men fought and died in the decisive battle of the American Revolution. Some were blown apart by unseen artillery, and others bled to death after being bayoneted by an enemy who looked them in the eye.

For many of us, historic battles are abstract and distant, dry passages from a textbook, dates to be noted, strategies to be memorized. But here at Yorktown, history comes off the page and marches onto the killing fields, where in this very bunker a young man's future bled away.

What makes this poignant to me is that we were in Yorktown on a family outing. Tom was fifteen at the time, and, had he been alive in 1781, he likely would have been here, experiencing what today seems a noble and heroic cause but what at the time must have been unspeakable terror. Boys younger than him died here.

How many years does it take to dehumanize war, to wash the blood from the soil, to boil it down to a chapter of text?

Places like Yorktown Battlefield Park exist so that the human face of war is not forgotten. Here we can memorize dates and study strategy, but we can also get to know the people whose lives were interrupted by battle.

Yorktown Battlefield is part of Colonial National Historical Park, which also includes Jamestown Island. The two sites are linked by Colonial Parkway, a scenic byway closed to commercial traffic.

We decided to tour Yorktown Battlefield by bicycle. For one thing, we enjoy riding together as a family, and, for another, the bike seemed the perfect vehicle for negotiating the sixteen miles of tour roads. We could see most of it in a day and still get a little closer to the landscape than had we taken the car.

Yorktown Battlefield has two tour routes. The seven-mile battlefield tour covers the area where the British maintained their defensive lines against American and French forces, and a nine-mile encampment route covers an area where allied soldiers lived, set up artillery, and maintained headquarters.

The tour roads are perfect for biking—nicely paved and, for the most part, lightly traveled. Some sections near the visitor center intersect with state roads, however, so traffic is heavier and caution is called for. Most of the tour roads are one-way, making them even more bike-friendly.

The visitor center is probably the best place to begin a bike tour. There is ample parking, and you'll get more from your trip if you preface it with some time spent among the artifacts and interpretive displays. Maps and guidebooks are also available. A seven-day pass, required to tour the park, is on sale there.

Other stops along the tour route provide parking and have less traffic, but it still is a good idea to stop at the visitor center, purchase a pass, and learn from the displays. You can join the encampment route from Newport News Park by taking the spur to Washington's Headquarters off the five-mile park trail. Parking is provided at the campground at Newport News Park, where the trail begins.

The seven-mile battlefield tour has more automobile traffic, but it is rich in history. In October 1781 British general Cornwallis established a naval base just north of where the visitor center stands, reasoning that, if he could win in Virginia, other southern states would claim loyalty to the Crown.

But the British made a tactical error. General Washington moved his army south from New York and was joined by French troops under General Rochambeau. Meanwhile, Admiral deGrasse and his fleet sailed to the mouth of the Chesapeake, where they defeated the British Navy under Admiral Thomas Graves in the Battle of the Capes. As Washington and Rochambeau advanced, Cornwallis realized he was trapped. A naval blockade at the mouth of the bay prevented escape or help by sea.

The allied forces dug a siege line south of Cornwallis's forces and then began an artillery barrage. The battle lasted about a week and ended with troops fighting at close quarters in the redoubts and trenches just off the roadway.

Cornwallis met with allied leaders on October 17 at the Augustine Moore house to discuss terms of surrender. His troops laid down their weapons at Surrender Field two days later.

The encampment tour begins at Surrender Field, with traffic one-way to Washington's Headquarters. The road crosses a small ford here that usually is four to six inches deep. A footbridge is provided if you'd rather not bike through the water.

The roadway continues past a French cemetery, through artillery positions, and around a loop where soldiers were encamped. This route is alternately wooded and open, with little traffic, and it's a good place to see wildlife. A one-way return route to the visitor center intersects with the encampment tour and reaches park headquarters via Route 238.

Bicycling along the encampment route is a peaceful experience. We went during the summer, amid a dry spell, and butterflies followed us and landed on our water bottles to drink condensation. When we stopped along the roadside for lunch, a herd of deer emerged from the woods and watched us with curiosity.

Yet, we are mindful of events that happened here more than two centuries ago. There was horror, and there was heroism. Our nation's destiny was shaped on this soil.

Yorktown at a Glance

GETTING THERE
Yorktown is on the York River between Williamsburg and Newport News north of Interstate 64. You can take Colonial Parkway from Williamsburg or exit I-64 on Route 238 and follow the signs. For information contact Colonial National Historical Park, P.O. Box 210, Yorktown, VA 23690. Or visit www.nps.gov/colo on the Internet.

BICYCLE ALERT
Park officials say that the grounds are being damaged by people riding off the paved roadways. If you ride your bike in the park, stay on the roads and designated parking areas.

FEES
A seven-day pass costs four dollars and is required for adults over age sixteen. Other national park passes are also honored.

YORKTOWN BY FOOT
A walking tour of historic Yorktown begins at the visitor center and extends through the old part of town and along the York River. A brochure is available at the visitor center.

Mountain Biking Tidewater Style

Dogwood Trail in Waller Mill Park tests riders' skill and stamina

The trail ran downhill, crossed a narrow bridge, and then snaked its way up a steep, forested slope on the other side of the gorge. "The idea is to get your speed up going downhill and to use the momentum to help you climb the hill on the other side," said Don Peterson, who was coaching me in the finer points of mountain biking.

We were on the Dogwood Trail at Waller Mill Park in Williamsburg, a six-mile circuit that resembles a roller-coaster ride with trees, logs, bridges, and various other attention-getting devices. As I stood with Peterson on top of the bluff, I wasn't worried about climbing the hill on the other side; I was worried about missing the bridge, which was about two feet wide but appeared much narrower from my vantage point. The bridge spanned a little feeder stream leading to the Waller Mill Reservoir. If I miss it I'm part of the Waller Mill ecosystem, not a pleasant thought.

"Stay back on the bike going downhill, then move forward when you climb," said Peterson. "I'll tell you when to shift."

The bike gained speed rapidly as I descended. I shifted my weight back, hung on, and, following Peterson's advice, looked not at the bridge but at a point beyond it. Just as the bike reached maximum speed, my right hand reached instinctively for the rear brake. Not a good idea. I hit the bridge safely but lost speed and had little momentum for the hill climb to come.

"Thumb! Thumb!" shouted Peterson, meaning that I should downshift. My bike has a flip-shifter with two levers. The small lever, controlled by the index finger, shifts the derailleur into a higher gear; the larger lever operated by the thumb shifts to a lower gear. I needed all the torque I could muster if I was going to make it up the hill.

Which I nearly did.

The trail zigzags uphill, meaning that, in addition to supplying power to the pedals, you have to maneuver the bike. I made it about three-fourths of the way to the top when the front wheel collided with a root, and the bike came to a stop. I walked it the rest of the way and watched as Peterson gracefully glided down the hill, accelerated across the bridge, and pumped his way to the summit without breaking a sweat.

Oh well, I told myself, Peterson has an advantage. He built the trail.

Peterson is president of the Eastern Virginia Mountainbike Association, whose members over the past eight years have built some twenty-seven miles of mountain bike trail in the Tidewater region. The Waller Mill trail is one of the best, Peterson says, a blend of twisting trail where technical skills are called for and fast, exhilarating hill rides designed to get the adrenaline flowing.

Peterson is a bike shop owner and tireless promoter of mountain biking as a family activity and an ideal way to stay fit and enjoy the outdoors. He invited Lynn, Tom, and me for a tour of the Waller Mill trail. We were joined by "Jumpin'" Joe Betz and Ben Holmes, both navy men who are expert riders.

At first glance, the phrase "Tidewater mountain biking" seems a contradiction in terms, given that the trail at Waller Mill is a few dozen feet above sea level. But the term "mountain biking" has become an all-encompassing one, referring to many different styles of all-terrain riding. There are no cliffs and boulders at Waller Mill, but there are hills, drops, jumps, and plenty of other obstacles to test one's agility, balance, and cycling skills.

Our experience with off-road biking had been limited to rather gentle trails such as those at First Landing State Park, Back Bay/False Cape, and various rails-to-trails venues around the state. So our first look at a steep downhill was a bit intimidating. "The trail is not for the meek," Peterson said, "but there is little about it that is really dangerous. Most of the time you're going slow enough that if you do have an accident you're not likely to get hurt."

Peterson said the trail is designed for mountain bikes with wide, knobby tires, and, preferably, with front suspension. Approved bike helmets are required.

We began our ride on a new section of trail, a one-mile circuit that winds through thick woodland. The trail is narrow, rooted, and contains numerous twists and turns but few hills and obstacles. "This is a warm-up trail," says Peterson. "It's technical in that it tests your bike-handling skills, your balance and agility, but it's not fast. That will come later."

The fast portion of the trail is the older section, one that, with a few alterations, has been in existence for some ten years. Here we get the swooping hills, the twists and turns, the jumps, and obstacles such as logs placed at a ninety-degree angle to the trail.

Good riders such as Peterson, Betz, and Holmes negotiate the trail effortlessly, using the downhill sections to gain momentum for the uphills. Betz, who has ridden competitively in Europe while in the navy, can make a bicycle defy gravity. I "bulldoze" my way over obstacles. Betz launches his bike into the air as he approaches, clears the obstacle without touching, and lands neatly with the rear wheel touching down first.

Tom quickly takes to the trail, "getting air" over the various jumps and obstacles, ignoring the temptation to ride the brakes going downhill. He flushes with pride and embarrassment as the older riders praise his skills.

But for Lynn and me, the first few miles of the ride deal more with survival than with skill. The uphill sections are particularly challenging, especially after a conservative descent in which most of our momentum was lost.

"You have to relax," said Peterson. "Most people aren't used to riding a bike down steep hills or over obstacles, and they tense up. But trust your bike. It was designed for this sort of thing, and it wants to stay upright."

After a few downhill runs and clearing a few jumps, we began to see Peterson's point. The bike can handle it, so relax and enjoy the ride. Soon we were running brakelessly down hills and then pumping our way up the next hillside, stopping now and then for a panoramic view of Waller Mill Reservoir.

At six miles, however, we were ready for a rest and some lunch. While six miles on a road bike is considered a short ride, six miles over hilly, challenging terrain provides a strenuous workout.

"Mountain biking is great for cardiovascular fitness," said Peterson. "It gets your heart rate up, and it works most of the major muscle groups. Plus it improves your balance and agility, the things we begin to lose as we age."

But is it safe?

Consider that if you're a road rider you're sharing your bikeway with vehicles that weigh two tons, travel at sixty miles per hour, and pass only a few feet from you.

With that in mind, those hills at Waller Mill are not intimidating at all.

Tidewater Mountain Biking at a Glance

WHERE TO RIDE IN TIDEWATER

Waller Mill Park is in Williamsburg. From I-64 take exit 238, turn left at the top of the off ramp, then turn right onto Rochambeau Drive at the light. At one and one-fourth mile turn left onto Airport Road, then turn left into the park. Dogwood Trail is directly across from the park entrance.

Harwoods Mill in Newport News Park has three trails designated for novice, advanced, and expert riders. Total distance is about five miles. From I-64 take exit 258 (Route 17 North) to Oriana Road, turn left, and the park is about one mile down on the left. The trail begins three hundred yards beyond the parking lot.

York River State Park in Williamsburg offers a variety of trails, some flat and easy, others challenging. From I-64 take exit 231B. Go one-half mile to Moss Side Road and turn right. At the yield sign bear right and take Riverview Road for one and one-half miles and follow signs to the park.

FOR MORE INFORMATION

Contact the Eastern Virginia Mountainbike Association at P.O. Box 7553, Hampton, VA 23666.

Chippokes Plantation State Park

*Along the James River, we go
riding with eagles*

The beach, the bikes, and bald eagles. A perfect formula for a memorable outdoor experience.

Tom and I decided to take off on a summer weekday and explore Chippokes Plantation State Park near Surry. Chippokes is on the James River less than an hour from Suffolk, and it probably qualifies as one of those local jewels that goes unnoticed and unappreciated by many who live in Tidewater.

Tom and I decided to explore the park by bicycle, taking advantage of the bike paths and the lightly traveled paved roads that run through forest and farmland. We began at the park headquarters at an overlook on the south side of the river and took College Run Trail, which runs along the James, to the plantation house in the eastern section of the park.

The trail runs downhill from the bluff, and soon we were at the level of the river and decided to take a look at the narrow beach, which was only a few feet from the trail. Shell fragments littered the beach—clams, scallops, oysters, and many others—and in the distance a small catamaran was making for land. In the opposite direction, a man and woman dozed in beach chairs while their dog waded in the shallow water. On a beautiful summer morning, we were the only people around.

Tom pointed out a bird drifting over. "Isn't that a bald eagle?" he asked.

Probably an osprey, I thought. But then I got a better look and noticed that the bird was much larger than an osprey, and then I saw the white head and tail. Not a bad way to begin a ride, we agreed: a quiet beach, a well-maintained trail, and a bald eagle soaring overhead.

Chippokes Plantation State Park offers bike and equestrian trails, the beach, a campground, and a swimming pool. But it also is a working farm and has been since 1619, making it one of the oldest continuously cultivated properties in the country. The historic Jones-Stewart mansion with its formal garden is in the eastern portion of the park, and River House and a multitude of barns and service buildings provide evidence that Chippokes is not just a park but a productive agricultural operation.

Corn was growing in fields along Cedar Lane, a narrow, paved road where three former tenant houses now serve as guest cabins. Near the mansion house, a Farm and Forestry Museum gives visitors a feel for what farm life might have been like more than a century ago. There are farm implements, tools, kitchenware, and much more.

Tom and I found that bicycles are the perfect vehicle for exploring Chippokes. College Run Trail, named for a nearby creek, is a narrow, paved roadway connecting the park office with the farm center. From there, the James River Trail and Lower Chippokes Creek Trail run through farmland and pasture to the banks of the James and Lower Chippokes Creek. Here the trail doubles as a farm lane, packed clay with the occasional wet-weather puddle.

While the dedicated bicycle trails are not long—less than four miles—the paved roads at Chippokes provide a pleasant additional ride. From the park entrance, the road leads past the campground and swimming pool to the park office, and from there to the Farm and Forestry Museum and the Jones-Stewart mansion and then through farm fields to a park exit on Virginia Route 634.

A ride at Chippokes provides a combination of natural and human history. The park includes eight thousand feet of shoreline along the James River, nearly nine hundred acres of forest, a similar tract of leased farmland, and about two hundred acres of wetlands. This diverse habitat supports twenty-four species of threatened or endangered animals and also provides nesting sites for bald eagles.

The human presence at Chippokes begins with the Native Americans who farmed and hunted here. Capt. William Powell acquired a grant to the property in 1619 but was killed in a raid on Chickahominy Indians in 1623. The farm later was owned by Gov. William Berkeley and Col. Phillip Ludwell, both prominent Virginians in the years prior to the Revolution. Albert Carroll Jones, a farmer from Isle of Wight County, bought the property in 1838 and built the brick mansion in 1854.

The plantation came under state ownership in 1967 when it was donated by Mrs. Evelyn Stewart in memory of her husband, Victor, who had purchased the property in 1918 and had grown a variety of crops and raised livestock on the farm. Mr. Stewart died in 1965, and the plantation was given to the state to be used as a park and maintained as a working farm so that visitors could experience day-to-day farm life.

Chances are Mrs. Stewart did not have bicyclists in mind when she made this generous gift to the people of Virginia nearly thirty-five years ago. But the roads and the trails at Chippokes provide cyclists and other visitors with a special experience: to visit an authentic, working Tidewater plantation and to ride with eagles.

Chippokes Plantation State Park at a Glance

GETTING THERE

Chippokes Plantation State Park is on the south bank of the James River on Route 634 east of the town of Surry. Take Route 10 west from Suffolk, or, from the peninsula, take Route 31 in Williamsburg, cross the James on the Scotland ferry, and continue on Route 31 to Surry. In Surry, take Route 10 east to Route 634, where there is a sign for the park entrance.

STAYING THERE

The park offers thirty-two campsites plus three rental cabins that are usually booked well in advance. Numerous accommodations are available in the Williamsburg area. South of the James, Surry offers overnight accommodations as well as the well-known Surrey House Inn, which specializes in traditional Virginia dishes such as peanut soup, soft crabs, country ham, and barbecued ribs. Riders will come away from the inn well fortified for the trails of Chippokes.

Biking Mathews County

Through the woods and to the water,
some of the best biking in Virginia

Could Mathews County be Virginia's best for bike-riding? A lot of people think so, including Doug Ellis, a veteran cyclist who is associate director of BikeWalk Virginia, a Williamsburg nonprofit organization whose mission is to promote biking, bicycle safety, and walking.

"Mathews is an ideal place to ride, especially if you're new to road riding and don't want to tackle the hill country of the western part of the state," said Ellis. "It's a rural county with nicely paved back roads, easy terrain, and wonderful scenery. A lot of counties fit that description in Tidewater Virginia, but Mathews has this wonderful system of interconnected back roads, many of which wind through forests and end up on the water somewhere."

Ellis's employer, BikeWalk Virginia, sponsors a bike tour of Mathews County each spring. The Tour de Chesapeake attracts hundreds of riders, many of whom come back each May to rediscover the charms of cycling flat, little-traveled roads that cross forests and salt marshes and end up at a secluded beach.

Lynn and Tom and I discovered Mathews County on one of the BikeWalk Virginia tours. We traveled back roads we never would have explored by car, investigated out-of-the-way coves, and took a

side trip by boat on the East River. We even enjoyed a lunch of barbequed chicken served by the local Ruritan club.

"One of the goals of our organization is to promote bike riding
as a safe, healthy way of exploring the countryside," said Ellis, "and
Mathews County is a good example of that. It's a little off the beaten
path, but it has all these great nooks and crannies that are perfect for
exploring by bike."

Our family spent the weekend in Mathews County, riding in the
Tour de Chesapeake on Saturday and staying over on Sunday for a
self-guided ride on Gwynn's Island. We pulled into Mathews County
late Friday afternoon, just in time to check into our hotel on Gwynn's
Island, and then headed over to Thomas Hunter Middle School in
Mathews for registration and the traditional pre-ride dinner of
spaghetti and salad.

Hunter Middle School serves as the headquarters for the ride,
and classrooms were put into use for bike safety classes, basic bike
mechanics, and displays of bicycling accessories. The Saturday ride
began with breakfast served in the school cafeteria, and then some
one thousand of us fanned out across the county on circuits ranging from fifteen miles to a metric century (sixty-two miles).

It was chilly and breezy when we left the parking lot, one of those
typical May mornings that begin with scuttling clouds hanging low,
a combination of sunshine and overcast, and the promise of changing weather. We packed extra jackets and headed out of town, hoping for warmth.

After a mile or two we got into a pedaling rhythm and began gen-
erating a little body heat. The jackets could have stayed in the car.
Two miles was also about what it took for us to discover a Mathews
County advantage other than flat terrain and light traffic. The county
is heavily forested, so even on a breezy day you're sheltered most of
the time. We encountered a few headwinds, but these were brief.
Either we'd pass through a forest or the road would change direction
and suddenly we'd have the wind behind us.

We signed up for a ride of thirty-four miles and were given a map
of the county with our circuit highlighted. The ride began and ended
at the school but took us through some fine Mathews County coun-

tryside. Soon after leaving the town of Mathews we were on our way out Tabernacle Road, passing pine woods and salt marsh, following a narrowing two-lane road that ended at a breezy beach where Mathews County meets the Chesapeake Bay. We saluted the Chesapeake with an energy bar and lemonade, then headed back across the peninsula to Williams Wharf, where lunch was being served.

After putting away an inordinate amount of barbequed chicken and accessory items, we left the bikes behind and boarded a boat for a tour of the East River. It was a trip of about an hour, a nice interlude from pedaling and a thoughtful addition ride organizers have come up with. The ride back to Mathews was leisurely, and we ended the tour with fresh strawberry shortcake served on the courthouse lawn.

Before heading home on Sunday, we explored Gwynn's Island by bike, beginning at the marina, where kids were catching croakers off the dock. The two-lane road passes homes and country stores, ending at a campground on the north end of the island. Along the way, we made a stop at the Gwynn's Island Museum, housed in the former Shiloh Church, where a docent gave us a tour of the museum's eclectic collection of Mathews County artifacts. After a final stop for some local seafood, we were on the road again, looking forward to returning soon to explore more of Mathews County's back roads.

Mathews County at a Glance

GETTING THERE

Mathews County is on the Chesapeake Bay at the tip of the Middle Peninsula. From Interstate 64 in Newport News, take Route 17 to Gloucester, turn right on Route 3/14, and follow it to Mathews. To reach Gwynn's Island, take Route 198 north from Mathews, turn right on Route 223, and follow it across the Milford Haven bridge to Gwynn's Island.

STAYING THERE

Several motels and bed-and-breakfast establishments are in the Mathews area. For information contact the Mathews County Visitor Center at 877-725-4229, or visit the Web site at www.mathewsva.org.

TOUR DE CHESAPEAKE

The Tour de Chesapeake is usually held the third weekend in May, and approximately a thousand riders participate. Registration and cycling classes are held on Friday evening at Thomas Hunter Middle School, and the ride begins on Saturday morning. A pasta dinner is served Friday evening, and breakfast is served Saturday morning at the school. For more information visit the Web site at www .tourdechesapeake.org. For information on other rides and programs sponsored by BikeWalk Virginia, see the Web site at www .bikewalkvirginia.org.

Belle Isle State Park

For a price, you can be a country squire for a week

Most state parks have campgrounds, and some even have rustic cabins. Write a modest check to the commonwealth, and you can pitch your tent and spend a week fishing, biking, hiking, or turning over rocks to look for salamanders—whatever gets your pistons pumping.

Belle Isle State Park on Virginia's Northern Neck offers something a little different. Ever wanted to be a country squire? Ever wanted to sip a mint julep as you sit on the veranda and survey your sloping lawn, your ancient shade trees, your sweeping vista of the Rappahannock River, your hundreds of acres of corn and soybeans?

This is not your momma and daddy's state park. You won't find any F-150s with camper attachments shoehorned into an RV space. No dump stations. No bathhouses. No laundromats.

What we have here is Bel Air Plantation, a Georgian-style mansion with five bedrooms, a library, a full kitchen, fireplaces all over the place, and, of course, a veranda complete with shade trees and stunning waterfront view. This is the kind of place that, when you walk up to the front door, you expect some breathless little waif in a cream-colored dress to exclaim, "Y'all come on in. Miss Scarlett be down d'rectly."

And it can all be yours. For a week. For a weekend. You name it. Of course, the check you'll write to the commonwealth will be substantial rather than modest, but that's beside the point.

Let's say you and the family want to get away from the ugliness of the world and rough it lavishly for a week. Bring your bike, your canoe, your fishing tackle and bird guide. But also pack the tweed jacket, the silk tie, the Laura Ashley dress, the single-malt scotch. You can be the duke and duchess of Belle Isle for a week. The squire and squirette.

In 1992 Virginia voters approved a bond referendum to purchase more land for parks and recreational facilities. At the time, Belle Isle neck, with 733 acres and 7 miles of shoreline, was growing corn and soybeans but was anticipated to soon become another waterfront subdivision, sprouting rows of McMansions instead of rows of beans. Within a year it had become a state park.

Today the fields still grow beans and corn, but the bluffs overlooking the river have family picnic facilities instead of private residences. The farm roads have become bike routes and equestrian trails. The piney woods on Deep Creek have been saved, and a pair of eagles nest along the footpath leading to Brewer's Point. The whitewashed old frame building near the park entrance, once home to a tenant family, is now the park office. From there, you can go down Mud Creek Trail and launch your canoe in Mulberry Creek, a sheltered cove that makes up the northern boundary of the park.

"Belle Isle is essentially still a working farm," said Tim Shrader, the park manager. "We rent the cultivated land on a competitive bid basis, and we use conservation practices to protect the watershed. The park is nearly surrounded by water."

While Belle Isle does not allow camping, many other activities are encouraged. There are trails for hiking, biking, and horseback riding. The trails are hard-packed clay and gravel and are uniformly flat, making them easily accessible for beginning riders and those who have no desire to cover long distances. Four trails provide a ride of about five miles. A picnic area with rest rooms and concessions are on a point where Deep Creek meets the Rappahannock.

But the main attraction of the park is the water. Mulberry Creek defines the northern boundary, the Rappahannock is on the south, and Deep Creek is on the eastern side. "Mulberry Creek is a great place to explore by canoe or kayak," said Shrader. "If you go at high tide, you can get to the upper reaches of the creek and see a wide variety of wildlife. If you want to fish, the Rappahannock has great saltwater fishing. Depending on the season, you can catch croaker, spot, flounder, rockfish, and other species. You can go in a boat or fish from the bank."

Bicycles, canoes, and small motorboats are available for rent at the park office, and picnic shelters can be reserved in advance for groups.

Shrader admits, though, that, while the park offers good fishing and biking trails and exemplary wildlife watching, the star attraction is Bel Air mansion. "The mansion and the guest house are unique to Virginia state parks," he said. "They provide the personality of the park, and making these facilities available to the public is something special. The mansion is not a museum but a living part of a working farm. We enjoy having people come in and become residents, if only for a while."

Belle Isle at a Glance

GETTING THERE

Belle Isle State Park is in Lancaster County on the Northern Neck. From Tidewater, take U.S. Route 17 north from I-64. You can cross the Rappahannock at Tappahannock and drive south down Route 3, or you can cross the river from Greys Point to White Stone and drive north from Whitestone. The park is on Route 683.

STAYING THERE

Want to be a squire for a week? The mansion at this writing rents for $1,400 for a week, or $233 per night, with a two-night minimum. The guest house rents for $600 per week or $100 per night. Combination rates are available for large parties such as weddings, family reunions, and corporate retreats. Phone the park at 804-462-5030 for more information. For information on accommodations outside the park, contact the Northern Neck Tourism Council at 800-393-6180. Visit the Web site at www.northernneck.org.

BE SURE TO BRING

A mountain bike is needed for the dirt trails. The park rents single-speed boardwalk cruisers for the casual rider. Mulberry Creek is great for exploring by canoe or kayak, as is the Rappahannock shoreline if the wind is not blowing from the southwest. Canoes and small motorboats are rented at the park. If you enjoy watching wildlife, bring the binoculars and field guides. Eagles nest in the park, and an observation blind in a shallow cove off Deep Creek is a good place to photograph waterfowl in winter. The park will get plenty of migrating songbirds early in the spring.

Westmoreland State Park

Searching for fossils on an ancient oceanfront

I'm sitting in a rocking chair on the porch of cabin 25, bundled against the morning chill, sipping coffee and watching the sun rise over the Potomac River. The sky is purple, and the Maryland shoreline is ghostlike in the distance. The Potomac is glassy calm. In the morning light, it looks like a sheet of stainless steel, undulating slightly.

In another half hour the sun will be up and focused. My cabin, on a bluff on Horsehead Cliff, sits atop an ancient treasure. These cliffs are 15 million years old, and, during the previous geological high tide, they were deep beneath the ocean waves. In the Miocene sediment that makes up these cliffs, we find evidence from that time long ago: fossils of ancient animals and fish, teeth of sharks and rays long extinct.

With the morning sun spotlighting the cliffs and beach and with the tide ebbing, it would be a perfect time to go fossil-hunting along the Potomac.

I was at Westmoreland State Park on the Northern Neck, near the town of Montross. Westmoreland is one of Virginia's six original state parks, having opened in 1936. The park has campgrounds and various other amenities, but the real attraction are these cabins built on a bluff that once was two hundred feet beneath the sea, a landscape that for reasons unknown to me attracted a wealth of fossils several million years ago.

My plan was to finish my coffee, make a sandwich of peanut butter and strawberry preserves, and then hike Big Meadows trail, which meanders through a hardwood forest, down a slope to Yellow Swamp, and finally to the beach at the base of Horsehead Cliffs. I'd eat the sandwich and then use the plastic bag to stow any small treasures I might find.

I wanted an ancient shark tooth, a chomper that last saw use by a predator perhaps 25 million years ago. Around that time, this area was part of the continental shelf; the Atlantic beachfront was somewhere near Fredericksburg. When ancient sea creatures died, they were quickly buried in sediment that preserved them. This sediment, made up of compacted sand, silt, gravel, and clay, is the stuff of which Horsehead Cliffs is made.

Now and then, especially during a hard rain, fossils are washed from the exposed sediment and can be found on the narrow beach or in the shallow waters of the Potomac. The park allows surface finds, and visitors may use sifting tools such as colanders to search for artifacts. Digging, however, is prohibited.

As the sun rose, I made my peanut butter sandwich, stuffed it in my jacket pocket, and began the hike through the woods and down the bluff. It was a weekday morning, and I had the place to myself. Only one other cabin in the area had been occupied, and those folks had apparently made an early getaway.

The trail is hard-packed clay, well-marked, and in the first sections is fairly level. But then it turns to the north and begins a quick descent to sea level, a drop of about two hundred feet. At the base of the bluff, you can continue farther into Yellow Swamp or turn left and gain access to the beach. I stopped briefly at an observation tower overlooking the swamp and then went in search of ancient treasure.

The sun was shining on the exposed cliffs, which line the Potomac from Westmoreland State Park east to neighboring Stratford Hall, birthplace of Robert E. Lee. The trail enters the beach at one of its wider areas, where at low tide there may be twenty to thirty feet of sand separating the vegetated upland and water. At some points, the Potomac laps against the cliffs, even at low tide.

Unlike the sandy ocean beaches of Tidewater, the Potomac beach was littered with thousands of stones, most of which were born in the Appalachians, weathered by thousands of years of ice and rain, and finally washed down to the piedmont, eventually to migrate to the coast. I picked several up and admired their shape and color, then returned them to the beach.

Living on the Atlantic coast, where stones are rare, we have come to appreciate their aesthetic values. These were smoothed and rounded by years of tumbling in streams; they were polished by moving water and sand. And then I found a fragment of a huge shell, a scallop, I thought, that must have been thousands of years old. And I found bits and pieces of what appeared to be bone, but hardened to a rock-like texture, fossilized.

I walked along the beach to the base of the cliff, where the water lapped under it. I felt the surface. It was smooth, rock-like in a way, although much more fragile. I saw no fossils, only strings and shards of plant root, exposed during a recent storm.

In two hours of searching, I found more shells, more bone-like fossils, and many more interesting stones. But no shark teeth. Scott Flickinger, the park manager, blamed it on the weather. "It's been dry," said Flickinger. "You need to come back after we've had a good rain and northeast wind."

I'm planning on it, Scott. Put me down for cabin 25.

Westmoreland at a Glance

GETTING THERE

Westmoreland State Park is six miles west of the town of Montross on Route 3 in Westmoreland County. From Tidewater, take U.S. Route 17 to Tappahannock, then Route 360 to Warsaw. Take Route 3 to the park.

STAYING THERE

The state park offers campgrounds, housekeeping cabins overlooking the Potomac, and a conference center for group retreats. You can make reservations by calling 800-933-PARK, or visit the Web site at www.dcr.state.va.us for more information.

AND WHILE YOU'RE THERE

There are many historical sites in the area, including the Washington and Lee birthplaces next door and Monroe's birthplace near Colonial Beach. For information on area accommodations and attractions, contact the Northern Neck Tourism Council at P.O. Box 1707, Warsaw, VA 22572. Visit the Web site at www.northernneck.org.

Caledon Natural Area Preserve

In an old-growth forest on the Potomac River, the eagles gather

Boyd's Hole Trail is a 3.5-mile loop beginning and ending at the visitor center at Caledon Natural Area. At roughly its halfway point, a short spur breaks off the main trail and goes down to a narrow beach on the Potomac River. If you want to see bald eagles, this could be the best place in Virginia to do so.

I was standing on the beach recently with Annette Bareford and Sammy Zambon of the Virginia Department of Conservation and Recreation. Two eagles were foraging a short distance off the shore. I looked northward down the beach and saw another pair perched high in a pine tree. We moved a little farther down the shoreline and saw four more.

"I never thought the day would come when seeing bald eagles in Virginia would be commonplace," I said.

"It's still pretty special, though," Bareford replied.

Eagles are common here along the southern shore of the Potomac for two major reasons. It's good eagle habitat, with lots of tall pines and hardwoods right along the shoreline, perfect for nest-building and for perching while waiting for a meal to appear. And state and federal wildlife officials have taken precautions to protect a large section of waterfront, which in northern Virginia has been under increasing pressure for development.

Because of its old-growth hardwood forest, Caledon has been designated a National Natural Landmark, and it has two missions: to protect bald eagle habitat and to educate visitors about the natural history of our national bird. Considering that Caledon is only about thirty-five miles, as the eagle flies, from our national capital, those missions seem fitting.

Caledon is in King George County about twenty miles east of Fredericksburg, not far off the I-95 corridor. The natural area has 2,579 acres of undeveloped land, including 3.5 miles of Potomac shoreline. "It's key bald eagle habitat," said Zambon, the chief ranger at the park. "There is a dense forest along the shoreline, some of it old-growth, and because it is not developed, the eagles can pretty much go about their business undisturbed. Plus, the prevailing wind and current here move flotsam toward the beach. So if a fish were to die offshore in the Potomac, it likely would wash up here and become food for a bald eagle."

The public education portion of Caledon's mission is met through a combination of public programs and field trips, interpretive displays at the visitor center, and a system of trails that introduce visitors to the natural habitat. To protect the eagles during nesting season, however, Boyd's Hole Trail is closed to individual hikers from April through September, and a thousand-foot no-boating zone is enforced along the nesting and perching area. Group trips are conducted by park rangers during this period.

The American bald eagle is one of those success stories that could instead have been a tragedy. Zambon said the eagles were once plentiful in the Chesapeake Bay area, with an estimated three thousand nesting pairs when the Europeans explored the bay in the early 1600s. Those numbers dropped precipitously in the 1950s and 1960s when pesticides such as DDT damaged the birds' ability to reproduce. Our national symbol was in danger of extinction in the lower forty-eight states until federal controls of pesticides and protection of habitat helped the population rebound.

Zambon said Caledon had about fifty eagles in the area last summer, although in some seasons staff naturalists have counted as many as ninety birds during the peak, which runs through June and July.

Zambon said the eagles mate for life and often use the same nest each year. "They begin the courtship process in November by re-building the nest, adding twigs and other material, and they lay their eggs usually in February," he said. "It takes five to six weeks for the eaglets to hatch, and when they do the parents are under a lot of pressure to provide for them. That's why we limit trail use beginning in April. The fledglings are ready to leave the nest in ten to eleven weeks, so in June and July we have the peak of the population, with the immature birds that nested here and other immatures that move into the area."

The immature eagles must learn to fly and fish in order to sur-vive, another reason the shoreline is closed during the summer, when the young birds are learning how to fend for themselves. "If they're disturbed, they flush and the adrenaline gets pumping," said Zambon. "They use a lot of energy that should be spent doing other things. So we bring groups in on a limited basis but restrict individ-ual access during this period."

The eagles do not get their mature plumage—the striking white head and tail—until their fifth year. The average life span is twenty-five years.

Caledon, named for a region in England, was donated to the state in 1974 by Ann Hopewell Smoot in honor of her late husband, Lewis Egerton Smoot. The historic Smoot home now serves as a visitor center, with a gift shop, staff offices, and a large interpretive display featuring the natural history of the bald eagle.

Caledon at a Glance

GETTING THERE
Caledon Natural Area is on the Potomac River about twenty miles east of Fredericksburg on Route 218.

STAYING THERE
Accommodations are available in the Fredericksburg area as well as King George County. Camping and housekeeping cabins are avail-able at Westmoreland State Park, about a half hour away. Contact

the Fredericksburg Visitors Center at 800-732-4732 or visit the Web site at www.fredericksburgva.net.

WHILE YOU'RE THERE

Eagles can be seen year-round at Caledon, with the highest concentrations during the summer. Five hiking trails are available year-round, with access limited to Boyd's Hole Trail during the summer. Caledon has a wide variety of educational programs, including eagle watches, hayrides, night walks, and astronomy sessions. Fall migratory bird hikes are scheduled for November. Call the park at 540-663-3861 for information.

Paddling the Pamunkey

*The river has abundant wildlife,
and George Washington slept here*

A small, squat, stable kayak is probably the best way to get around on the water, especially when the water is shallow, narrow, and twisty. Garrie Rouse and I were paddling the Pamunkey River and had taken a little side stream called Macon Creek. When it comes to narrow and twisty, Macon Creek could be called the pretzel of waterways. If you paddle fast enough up Macon Creek, you can meet yourself coming the other way.

Rouse is a botanist and river guide, and Macon Creek is one of his favorite places. It's a beautiful stream to paddle, in a rural setting within the Pamunkey Indian Reservation, and the freshwater marsh that lines this waterway is rich in plants and in the wildlife they attract. When Rouse does one of his environmental education sessions on the water, this often is where he heads, an area rich in both human history and natural history.

When Rouse and I went paddling recently, we launched our kayaks on an alcove of the Pamunkey called the Pocket. It was nearly high tide, and the river was wide and full; at low tide, with the water four feet lower, the main channel would have been lined with vegetation, which when we launched was visible just beneath the surface of the water.

"I've found that it makes life easier to schedule trips with the tides," said Rouse. "We'll paddle upriver with the rising tide, and then when the tide begins to ebb we'll circle around and make our way back. We'll paddle to Poplar Grove and up Macon Creek until we can't paddle anymore, and then we'll make our way back. It's a loop of about four miles."

Paddling the Pamunkey provides a study in contrasts. The river is wide here, narrowing only slightly as we made our way upstream to Poplar Grove. There were duck blinds constructed stilt-like on the open water; and along the edges, foraging in the shallows, we could see black ducks, mallards, and teal. Black vultures perched in tall pines that lined the river. The Pamunkey here is a wild place, with only a few reminders of civilization. It's hard to believe that Richmond is but forty or so miles away.

When we turned into Macon Creek the water went from wide to narrow, from straight to twisting, with countless little offshoots to explore, some barely able to accommodate the thirty-inch-wide boats. As a botanist, this is Rouse's kind of place. He nudged his kayak into a thick mat of grasses about three feet high and then began examining the tiny seed heads. "This is wild rice," Rouse said. "It's the reason these marshes are so rich in wildlife. The ducks we passed a while ago feed on it, as well as many kinds of songbirds."

As he spoke, a flock of red-winged blackbirds gathered in a grass thicket along the riverbank. Sparrows could be seen scurrying through the thick lower leaves. In the distance came a high-pitched, plaintive call I could not identify. "It's a sora," said Rouse. "These wild rice meadows are full of them, although they're rarely seen. The grasses provide a food source for them, as well as a place to hide."

A sora is a rail-like bird uncommon in the saltwater marshes of tidewater but frequently heard in these brackish and freshwater marshes well upstream from the Chesapeake. Although this section of the Pamunkey is strongly tidal, the salt content is very low, around 0.5 parts per thousand, Rouse said. The result is a tidal marsh that supports a wide diversity of plants and wildlife.

"The wider portions of the river are interesting, but the upper marsh has such a diversity of life," said Rouse. "If I take out a student group, I consider it an outdoor classroom. They can paddle the open water and enjoy getting a feel for the boat, but when we get up in here they begin to learn how life in the tidal marsh actually functions. The grasses produce seeds, which are eaten by ducks, songbirds, and soras. They also learn that the marsh is not a swampy, forbidding place but a natural system of great richness and beauty."

The area of the Pamunkey we paddled also has played its role in Virginia history. It is the land of native Virginians, the people of the Pamunkey tribe, and legend has it that George Washington met and fell in love with Martha Custis on this spot.

Rouse says the Washington-Custis story has several variations, but in general it goes like this: Mrs. Custis was a young widow who was visiting Colonel Chamberlayne's family at Poplar Grove when George Washington crossed the Pamunkey here in 1758, on his way to Williamsburg. He was invited by Colonel Chamberlayne to stay for the evening and was presented to Mrs. Custis, a twenty-six-year-old widow of some eight months. Washington apparently was smitten. He left the next day for Williamsburg, quickly attended to matters of state, and soon returned to Poplar Grove to attend to matters of the heart.

The Pamunkey at a Glance

GETTING THERE

The Pamunkey River separates New Kent and King William Counties on the Middle Peninsula, northeast of Richmond. The Pamunkey empties into the York River at West Point. Garrie Rouse has made arrangements with the Pamunkey tribe to operate guided tours and educational trips from the reservation. Contact him at Mattaponi Canoe and Kayak in Aylett, Virginia. The phone number is 800-769-3545. Visit the Web site at www.mattaponi.com.

AND WHILE YOU'RE THERE

Another interesting canoe/kayak day trip in the area is on the Mattaponi River, which separates King William and King and Queen Counties and also joins the York at West Point. Rouse leads a novice-level trip of 4.8 miles from Zoar State Forest north of Aylett to a Department of Game and Inland Fisheries boat landing near U.S. Route 360. The river here runs through forest rather than open marsh and is very scenic in spring and fall. The state maintains a hiking trail in Zoar State Forest, a good place to look for spring wildflowers.

Central Virginia and the Highlands

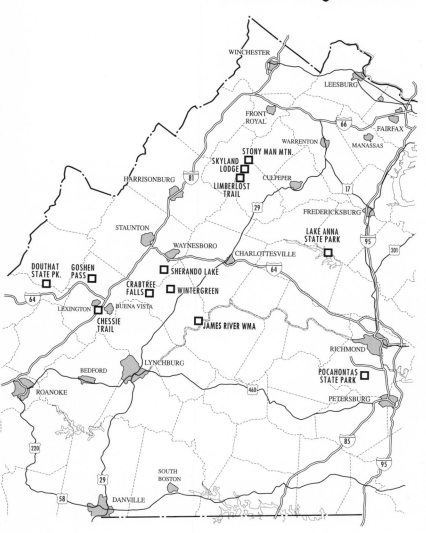

Pocahontas
State Park

*An island of green provides respite
from the interstate traffic*

When Pocahontas State Park was built, it was out in the country in what then was rural Chesterfield County. The state capital, some twenty miles to the north, seemed a world away, in character if not in distance.

In recent years, the capital has spread across Chesterfield in an invading army of strip malls and motels, gobbling up open land and converting it to asphalt. The I-95 corridor between Richmond and Petersburg is thickening at the waist, spreading east and west like a corpulent uncle unbuttoning his trousers after Thanksgiving dinner.

The area begs to be burped.

I wonder if this is what state officials had in mind years ago when they created Pocahontas State Park, which then was out in the country but now is an island of green amid congested traffic and asphalt.

We drove out to Pocahontas recently, taking Route 10 from Tidewater through the chemical plants of Hopewell, crossing under I-295 and I-95, and driving through Chester and Chesterfield to Route 655 and the entry to the state park.

Pass through the check-in, pay the student intern the three-dollar parking fee, and click the switch. Poof. The growling tractor-trailers are silent, the Formula One wannabes are stilled, and green again covers the earth.

Could those state park gurus in the 1930s have had such foresight? Could they have known how valuable this oasis would become, once surrounded by the needs of commerce and industry?

It truly is remarkable to drive through those gates, park the car, and discover how wonderful quiet can be. We're surrounded by city and suburb, by millions of people, and yet there's a sense of peace. We're the hole in the donut.

Tom and I wanted to ride the bikes, and Pocahontas has some great trails. Old Mill Bicycle Trail begins near the entrance gate and winds its way around the park in a loop of almost seven miles. Foot trails connect with the bike trail to provide access to the old mill site, Beaver Lake, and the dam that creates the lake.

Tom's favorite is the series of mountain bike trails constructed and maintained by volunteers of the Virginia Mountain Bike Association, in cooperation with the park. There are four of them, each color-keyed beginning with the green-flagged novice trail and progressing to the red-flagged trail intended for advanced riders.

The mountain bike trails are spurs that intersect Old Mill Trail along the northern portion of the loop. The trails are single-track and technical, with lots of maneuvering, overcoming obstacles, and climbing and descending hills. The four trails total about ten miles.

Old Mill Bicycle Trail is a hard-packed clay-and-gravel roadway that winds through the forested areas of the park. It is not a mountain bike trail as such, but loose gravel and exposed roots make it questionable for road bikes. The trail has lots of hills, so the seven-mile ride provides a good cardiovascular workout, especially if you're used to riding on flat terrain.

The trail literally bisects the grounds of the Civilian Conservation Corps Museum, which pays tribute to the young men of the Depression era who helped build Pocahontas and other parks in Virginia. Indeed, the museum is housed in a cabin built by the CCC crew in the late 1930s.

Just down the park road from the CCC Museum is the extensive swimming pool complex and the Heritage Center, which is used for exhibits, displays, and performances.

Incredibly, considering the number of people who live within a thirty-mile radius of the park, there were very few visitors when Tom and I spent a recent weekday there. We met one couple on the mountain bike trails, another on Old Mill Trail. A ride through the camping areas indicated that the park was being used and enjoyed but was far from crowded. Many of the camping spots were vacant.

The park offers sixty-five sites with electric and water hookups, as well as picnic shelters, a conference center, and an outdoor amphitheater. Guided programs include a hike around Beaver Lake, a night hike, and canoe trips on Swift Creek Lake.

Tom and I biked the trails, visited the CCC Museum, and walked around Beaver Lake. The only negative aspect of the trip came at the end, when it was time to put the bikes on the rack, stash the helmets and water bottles, and get back on the highway.

Pocahontas State Park at a Glance

GETTING THERE

Pocahontas State Park is between Richmond and Petersburg just west of the town of Chester. Take Route 10 to Chester, turn left on Route 655 (Beach Road), and follow the signs to the park. There is a modest parking fee and a fee for use of the pool.

STAYING THERE

The park offers campsites with hookups at eighteen dollars per night. Numerous motels and restaurants are located along the Chester exit at I-95. The park is about ten miles west of Chester.

WHILE YOU'RE THERE

Richmond and Petersburg offer many historic attractions. If you visit the area from Tidewater, consider taking Route 5 from Williamsburg and visiting the James River plantations along the way. Sherwood Forest, Evelynton, Westover Gardens, Berkeley, and Shirley Plantation are all just off Route 5. Cross the James via the Route 106 bridge and pick up Route 10 east of Hopewell.

Lake Anna

*A state park is sitting on
a gold mine*

On a Sunday morning in 1825 some Orange County children were returning home from church, no doubt with a fried-chicken dinner on their minds. They took a shortcut through a local judge's property, and one of them stumbled over a shiny rock. Ah yes, it was gold.

These children, fresh from Sunday school, touched off Virginia's version of a gold rush, as men, women, and children flocked to the Piedmont to seek their fortunes. Little is known today of Virginia's gold rush, but prior to the discovery of gold in California in the mid-nineteenth century, Virginia was the third-largest producer in the United States, sending more than $1.5 million in gold to the United States mint.

On a crisp fall day I headed off into the woods of Spotsylvania County to see if those earlier prospectors might have missed something. Thomas Jefferson once found a four-pound rock along the Rappahannock River that had seventeen pennyweight of gold in it. I could do with a rock like that. That would cover a car payment or two.

With me were Annette Bareford and David Floyd of the Virginia Department of Conservation and Recreation, Division of State Parks, owner of more than two thousand acres of gold-laden Spotsylvania County, which over the years has had twenty-three working mines. Lake Anna State Park, known to many for its fine swimming beach, excellent fishing, and rolling hillsides, is literally sitting on top of a gold mine.

We met at the park headquarters, and Floyd, the assistant park manager, led us along a wooded trail in an area called Pigeon Run in the northern portion of the park. Fittingly, the leaves that still clung to the trees were the finest shade of gold, and in a gentle breeze with the sun behind them, they would shimmer like jewels. Underfoot, ferns were still green and lush, providing a nice visual complement to the changing leaves.

Floyd stopped at an area deep in the woods that obviously had seen a human presence many years ago. The hillside was pock-marked with craters, and the remains of stone columns or supports stood in a line along the slope. Shards of rusting metal could be seen here and there among the leaf litter.

"This was the site of the Goodwin gold mine," said Floyd. "The Goodwins owned the property as far back as the late 1700s, but we believe the peak years for the mine were from 1881 to 1887."

The Goodwin mine was mechanized, so, instead of a team of prospectors searching for gold chips in a pan filled with water and ore, the hard work was done by a steam engine. Floyd said the Good-win mine had a shaft ninety-five feet deep, with another tunnel two hundred feet long extending from it. A head frame above the shaft held a bucket on a pulley that transported mine workers and ore in and out of the mine.

Once ore was extracted, it was crushed in a machine called a stamp mill and then washed down a sloping table fitted with ripples, which trapped the gold particles. "It was a fairly straightforward operation," said Floyd. "Gold is heavier than other metals, so it settles out and separates. It's the same principle individuals use in panning gold."

As Floyd explained the mechanical process of separating gold from quartz and other minerals, my eye was drawn to rocks that covered the old mine site. Could there still be a few ounces that the earlier prospectors had missed? I picked up a few stones, examined them carefully, and decided I had better be prepared to write a check to cover the next car payment.

Back at the visitor center, Floyd showed us an artist's rendering of the 1880s gold mine and demonstrated how early prospectors found and extracted gold from the North Anna River. Lake Anna is probably Virginia's only state park that offers gold panning as an interpretive program. Indeed, the park's plan is to turn the old mine into an educational resource and have guided group tours for visitors wanting to learn more about Virginia's gold rush.

"We have the signs made, and we've built replicas of some of the equipment that was used," said Floyd. "The only issue now is one of safety. We know there are mine shafts down there, and before we start bringing in vans loaded with school children, we want to make sure the area is safe. We're in the process of doing that right now."

On the trail at Pigeon Run, the only gold I found was clinging to the hickories and oaks that dotted the hillside, and soon even those nuggets would be gone with the wind. And I wondered about the hopes and dreams of the people who worked in this landscape more than a century ago. The work had to have been grueling, but the rewards must have been exhilarating. Yet, one day it came to an end.

And now the shafts have caved in, the stonework is covered with leaves and moss, the hardware is pitted and rusting. But the mine site at Pigeon Run seems more of a memorial than a relic, a testimony to the hopes, dreams, and hard work of a special people in a special time.

Lake Anna at a Glance

GETTING THERE

Lake Anna is southwest of Fredericksburg, and the state park is on the north side of the lake in Spotsylvania County near the community of Bells Cross Roads.

STAYING THERE

The state park has no campground or cabins, although these are in the planning stage, awaiting funding. There are a number of private campgrounds, motels, and restaurants in the area. For information visit the Lake Anna Web site at www.lakeannaonline.com.

AND WHILE YOU'RE THERE

Lake Anna State Park has more than twenty-three hundred acres to explore, including thirteen miles of trails for hiking, biking, and horseback riding. A boat launch, visitor center, bathhouse, snack bar, and swimming beach are on the lake. For more information contact the park at 6800 Lawyers Road, Spotsylvania, VA 22553. The phone number is 540-854-5503. Some facilities are open only on a seasonal basis.

Skyland Lodge

*George Pollock's resort has been
a family favorite for generations*

Skyland Lodge has always been a special place for our family. My parents spent their honeymoon there, and some years later I got my first taste of hiking mountain trails at Skyland. So it has served generations of our family, giving us an appreciation for the wilderness of the Blue Ridge.

Skyland is in the Shenandoah National Park near the town of Luray and is one of our favorite places for taking an outdoor vacation in a manner that might be called roughing it smoothly.

Skyland was built in the late 1800s by a visionary named George Freeman Pollock, who loved exploring the ridges and valleys of the Blue Ridge Mountains in Page County. Pollock's father was a principal in a New York copper-mining company that owned more than five thousand acres east of Luray, and, when efforts to extract copper proved futile, he sent George to the area to see if the land might be of any other value.

The younger Pollock, who was sixteen at the time, became fascinated with the beauty and wilderness of the Blue Ridge; and, being a rather sociable young man, he decided that the breezy ridges, the magnificent views, and the cool springs would be the perfect setting for entertaining summer guests. He convinced his father and his business partners to press forward with plans for a resort on Stony Man Mountain that would become Skyland.

Skyland became a popular summer retreat in the early 1900s, and Pollock became a colorful, if eccentric, host. He awakened his guests at seven each morning by playing "Reveille" on his bugle, and he kept a bathtub full of snakes, which he would show off at dinner. But the outdoors lured visitors to Skyland—the hiking and horseback trails, the springs, the waterfalls, the relief from the oppressive summer heat of the city.

Shenandoah National Park was dedicated in 1933, and Skyland has become a focal point for exploring the park. As in Pollock's day, it remains a fairly rustic resort. The outdoors and the views provide the entertainment, so there are no televisions in the cabins, no telephones or swimming pools, and a fitness center would seem not only out of place but redundant.

The cabins at Skyland have double beds, a desk and chairs, dresser, coffeemaker, and a modern bath. Most are wood-paneled and have a small deck that overlooks the valley below. Deer browse the grounds like contented farm animals, and black bears are frequently seen along the trails.

The dining room, "Pollock Room," is finished in natural wood, with one wall of glass that on clear days offers a commanding view of the valley below. On days when the valley is not so clear, you can sip your morning coffee and watch the cloud formations slowly change form like aerial amoebae.

The dining room is not pretentious, and the food is something like Grandma might have cooked after church on Sunday: fried chicken, grilled steak and pork chops, turkey and dressing, blueberry pancakes, blackberry cobbler. Portions are served with the assumption that you are spending the better part of the day hiking the trails and thus need to be fortified.

And the trails are the lure of Skyland. Some are short—less than a mile—and others can keep you walking all day. The Appalachian Trail runs through Shenandoah National Park and Skyland, frequently intersecting with side trails that lead to a waterfall, a cool spring, or a rock outcropping that provides a sweeping view.

Miller's Head Trail is a relatively short hike that begins just east of the Skyland cabins, but it offers a great view of the valley to the west, and in the evening the lights of Luray make the valley look like Christmas. Stony Man Trail, on the north part of the property, is a little longer, but the view from the top of Stony Man Mountain is well worth the walk. Limberlost Trail, with a grove of old-growth hemlocks, is a loop of a little over a mile and is handicapped accessible. If you don't feel like walking, the Skyland stables will arrange a horseback ride for you.

For more than a century, Skyland has encouraged guests to get up, get out, and get active. George Pollock no longer begins the day with a bugle call, but the trails, the shady springs, and the remote waterfalls invite you to lace up your hiking boots and begin exploring.

Skyland at a Glance

GETTING THERE

Skyland Resort is in Shenandoah National Park between mileposts 41 and 42. From the south and east take I-64 to Waynesboro and drive north on the Skyline Drive, a distance of sixty-four miles. An alternative would be to take U.S. Route 33 west of Richmond and access the Skyline Drive west of Standardsville at the Swift Run Gap entrance station. Skyland is about twenty-five miles north of the Route 33 intersection. From the north, enter the park at Front Royal and drive south on Skyland Drive forty-one miles to Skyland.

STAYING THERE

The cabins at Skyland are comfortable but not fancy. They do not have TV or phone. Camping is available in Shenandoah National Park, and motels and restaurants are numerous in the Luray area. Big Meadows lodge is approximately ten miles south of Skyland on the Skyline Drive. Phone 800-999-4714 for information on both Skyland and Big Meadows Lodge. Phone 540-999-3500 for park information.

WANT TO KNOW MORE?

Many guides are available to the trails of Shenandoah National Park. Our favorite is Henry Heatwole's *Guide to Shenandoah National Park*. Map 10 of the Appalachian Trail published by the Potomac Appalachian Trail Club covers the Skyland and Big Meadows area.

Limberlost Trail

This trail provides an unlimited wilderness experience

All of us have physical limitations. I can jog three miles, but I can't do a marathon. I can log twenty-five miles on the bike, but a century ride is beyond me. I'm not complaining. In my mid-fifties, I consider myself lucky that my physical limitations are fairly unconfining.

Many of us miss out on outdoor experiences because of our limitations, be they age, physical injury, or medical conditions that turn ordinary activities into physical challenges. Fortunately, Virginia has many places where quality outdoor experiences are available to folks who, for whatever reason, have severe physical limitations. One of the best is Limberlost Trail in Shenandoah National Park near Luray.

Limberlost is a 1.3-mile circuit that meanders through an oak forest, a dense thicket of mountain laurel, and a stand of old-growth hemlocks nearly four hundred years old. The trail is gently sloping and has a surface of hard-packed crushed greenstone, making it accessible to people with mobility limitations. The diversity of habitat in a relatively small area makes it possible to see a variety of wildlife and experience different aspects of a forest.

Our family hiked Limberlost with park ranger Jim Sluiter, who led a group of about fifteen on a leisurely hike through the oaks and hemlocks. Among our group were novice hikers perhaps three or four years of age, others who were considerably more chronologically gifted, and some who had physical limitations such as severe visual impairment.

All of us enjoyed the hike, and many would not have gotten to spend a morning among the oaks and hemlocks were it not for this special path. A conventional hiking trail with loose rocks, steep climbs and descents, and unsure footing would have been impossible to navigate.

So Limberlost Trail opens up a small portion of mountain wilderness to those of us who might not otherwise be able to enjoy this experience. Credit for this goes not only to Shenandoah National Park but also to a large group of volunteers, most notably the Old Dominion Chapter of the Bell Atlantic Pioneers of America, who provided funding, materials, equipment, and thousands of hours of volunteer service to make the trail possible.

And Limberlost does provide a quality outdoors experience. My wife and I hiked the trail late on the afternoon before going with Ranger Jim and the group. A thunderstorm had just rumbled through, and we had the trail to ourselves. In an old apple orchard, birds were using the break from the rain to feast on emerging insects. We stopped for about ten minutes and saw a scarlet tanager, chickadees, a white-breasted nuthatch, black-and-white warbler, Kentucky warbler, eastern wood pewee, and a blue-gray gnatcatcher.

On an earlier hike we had seen a black-throated blue warbler, red-eyed and solitary vireos, and towhees. We also saw a red squirrel and two ribbon snakes making their way along the trail. Wildflowers are abundant in spring, summer, and fall. One new to me was the "doll's eye," named for obvious reasons.

But the stars of Limberlost Trail are the huge hemlock trees, old-growth timber that might have had roots in the soil here when Capt. John Smith arrived at Jamestown. And, of course, within this ancient and shady forest, there is a legend.

As we recently walked the path with park ranger Jim Sluiter, he told us of an attractive young woman named Addie Pollock and a man named Mr. Grim. A century ago, Mr. Grim owned the forest where the hemlocks grow. Addie Pollard lived nearby; her husband was George F. Pollock, founder of Skyland Lodge on Stony Man Mountain. Addie loved the mountain wilderness and frequently rode her horse through the hemlock grove, which at that time must have been even more special because the surrounding forest had been clear-cut.

One day Addie was riding through the hemlock grove and noticed that several of the giant trees had been marked with an axe, a signal that they were to be cut. Addie became very upset, contacted Mr. Grim, and offered to buy the timber rights to the eight marked trees for ten dollars each. A deal was struck, and Mr. Grim agreed to spare the marked trees.

But some time later, on another ride, Addie found that more trees bore axe marks. She again contacted Mr. Grim, offered ten dollars per tree, and he agreed to spare them. Eventually Addie spent more than a thousand dollars, but the grove of hemlocks was saved. She named the area Limberlost after a popular novel of the era, *The Girl of the Limberlost,* by Gene Stratton Porter.

As we walked through the hemlock grove, Sluiter pointed out one especially impressive tree. On one side of it, about four feet off the ground, was the ancient but unmistakable scar of an axe. Mr. Grim's mark lives on, but the hemlocks are the legacy of Addie.

Limberlost Trail at a Glance

GETTING THERE

Limberlost Trail is on the Skyline Drive at milepost 43, near Skyland Lodge. The trail is a 1.3-mile loop with a hard-packed surface of greenstone. White Oak Canyon Trail intersects with Limberlost and leads to White Oak Falls, a more difficult hike of about four miles. The park offers guided hikes on Limberlost Trail on a regular basis, and these provide a great introduction to the history and natural history of the area. Ask for information at the park entrance stations.

WILDLIFE ON THE TRAIL

Fall is a good time to see birds on the trail. Migratory birds such as warblers, tanagers, and thrushes will be coming through, and hawks can be seen from overlooks. The old apple orchard is probably the best place for seeing songbirds. Deer are plentiful along the trail, and there is the possibility of seeing a black bear.

BE SURE TO BRING

Binoculars and a good field guide are essential for bird-watching. The path is smooth and hard-packed, so comfortable walking shoes get the call over hiking boots. The trail is not long, but if you take your time and enjoy the sights, you might want to bring water and a snack.

Stony Man Mountain

Want to see a bear? This is the place to go.

The popular hook and bullet magazines have for years subsisted on three themes: how to kill a deer, how to catch a bass, and how to avoid being eaten by a bear. Bears have been on the cover of thousands of outdoor magazines, usually depicted in some moment of great drama. A plaid-shirted woodsman, armed only with a flashlight and a can opener, fends off a two-thousand-pound snarling, drooling, wild-eyed grizzly bear.

The bear on the trail ahead of us on Stony Man Mountain was not snarling and drooling, as far as I could tell. It appeared to be eating blueberries and did not seem especially fearsome. It looked like an overweight black Lab with thick legs.

Nevertheless, conditioned by too many summer afternoons as a boy reading outdoor magazines in the back of the drugstore, I slowly reached for my pocketknife. I became somewhat concerned when I found only the car keys and some small change, realizing I had left the knife in the kitchen sink, smeared with peanut butter.

But Tom had his trusty multi-use pocketknife, an amazing instrument that within seconds can transform itself from knife to can opener to pliers and more. He took the tool from its case, quickly manipulated it into the pliers configuration, and handed it to me.

Should the bear attack, I would go for the molars. A toothless bear is a friendly bear.

But the bear was no longer there. The blueberry thicket was empty. The bear had disappeared without a sound, silently retreating to the deeper woods, gone like a forgotten dream.

"Black bears are pretty shy," park ranger Jim Sluiter told me on a later hike on Stony Man Mountain. "They prefer to stay away from people. They will defend themselves if threatened, like any other animal, but they prefer to avoid humans. Just don't bother a sow if she has cubs."

The bear's almost mythical reputation, coupled with its shyness, make bear sightings special, especially for folks like us who live in an area where there are no bears. We had a great hike on Stony Man, enjoyed the wonderful view from the rock outcropping at four thousand feet, but what we'll remember most is the brief encounter with a shy animal that no doubt feared us more than we feared him.

Stony Man Mountain, the second-highest peak in Shenandoah National Park, is a good place to see black bears. Before we actually saw the bear, we found evidence of a bear-foraging expedition. Rotten logs were torn apart by a bear apparently searching for insects or grubs to eat. One tree had claw marks about six feet up the trunk.

Bears fare well here in Shenandoah National Park, with plenty of wilderness to explore in an area closed to hunting. Poachers killed many bears in the park several years ago, but a sting operation put most of the poachers out of business, and park rangers say the bears are enjoying a comeback.

Stony Man Trail is a short, easy hike, but it has a great deal to offer, including the possibility of seeing a black bear. It's a mile-and-a-half round trip, with the halfway point the rock outcropping that, on a clear day, provides a spectacular view of the valley below. The trail begins and ends near milepost 42 on the Skyline Drive, at the northern entrance to Skyland Resort.

When you reach the outcropping, you're actually standing on the face of the stony man. From an observation area farther north on the Skyline Drive, the face appears as the profile of a bearded man with a rather prominent nose. No one seems to know who made this observation and gave the mountain its name, but it's been around for more than a century at least. When George Pollock opened Skyland resort in the 1890s, he chose Stony Man and the view it presented of the valley as the site.

Bears seem to like Stony Man as well. Although the trails near the Skyline Drive have their share of human visitors, the bears seem to tolerate us, knowing that thousands of acres of less-accessible wilderness are just a short distance away.

When we drove to dinner on our last day at the park, we saw another bear ambling through a wooded area just off the Skyline Drive. I stopped the car and called to it. The bear stopped, regarded us briefly, and, apparently deciding that we were of little importance, shuffled up the hillside.

Stony Man Mountain at a Glance

GETTING THERE

The Stony Man Mountain trailhead is at the north entrance to Skyland near milepost 42. A parking lot is on the right just as you exit the Skyline Drive. The trail is about a mile-and-a-half round trip and is an easy walk.

LEARNING MORE

Stony Man Trail is a good place to learn about the natural and human history of the Shenandoah National Park. It is an interpretive trail, and a nicely illustrated guidebook is available at the trailhead. An impressive view of the valley can be enjoyed at Stony Man Cliffs, at an elevation of 4010 feet.

Mr. Crabtree's Falls

A mountain family homestead is now one of Virginia's most popular trails

It was just after dawn on the Blue Ridge Parkway, and I had the windows down, the heater on, and John Prine on the car stereo.

I like the smell of fallen leaves when it's early and still and a heavy dew is on the ground. Most things smell rotten when they decompose, but not leaves. They smell of earth, of stored sunlight, of photosynthesis in reverse.

John Prine's is good leaf-smelling music, simple and uncluttered; his voice is nasal but pleasant, Bob Dylan with the edges ground down.

I was headed for Crabtree Falls, eager to get an early start, my fanny pack filled with a camera, water bottle, and sandwiches made with crunchy peanut butter and fig preserves.

Crabtree Falls is near the community of Montebello and is about eight miles off the parkway on Route 56. I stopped in at the Montebello Country Store and said good morning to Madeline Grant, whose late husband was related to the Crabtrees, who lived on the mountain whose falls bear their name.

"If you go all the way to the top of the mountain, there's a meadow up there, and that's where the Crabtrees lived, along with several other families," she told me. "They would come down to the store every now and then and buy their sugar and salt and coffee. But they made a living up there on the mountain, raising crops and livestock. They settled there early, in the late 1700s or pretty quick afterwards."

The Crabtrees are gone now, although their name is still attached to the little creek that cascades down the mountain, as well as to the meadow that is atop it. The mountain, and the falls, are now part of George Washington National Forest, and the U.S. Forest Service maintains a three-mile trail that runs from a parking area on Route 56 to the top of the falls and to Crabtree Meadows.

I left Mrs. Grant, drove down Route 56 to the parking area at the base of the falls, and began my hike, thinking about Mr. Crabtree. I pictured him as a wiry old guy with a beard, faded overalls, a tattered hat, and a chaw of his own making in his left cheek. He was no stranger to hard work.

Although the Crabtree farmstead is long gone, I like to think about the human presence here. Today it consists of hikers like myself who come for a day to admire the cascading water as if it were a shrine, and then leave. But Mr. Crabtree lived and worked here. Would he, at the end of the day, sit by the tumbling water and admire this wonderful landscape he owned?

I strapped on my fanny pack, crossed the arched wooden bridge over the south fork of the Tye River, and began my hike up Crabtree Creek, which empties into the Tye in a rather spectacular fashion. It had been dry and the water level was low, but still the cascading water could be seen far up the mountainside.

Crabtree Falls is the highest waterfall east of the Mississippi. The parking lot is at an elevation of about eighteen hundred feet, and by the time you hike the three miles to the top of the falls and Crabtree Meadows, you're at three thousand feet, a climb of about twelve hundred feet.

Yes, the trail is steep. The forest service has thoughtfully provided rest stops, aka scenic overlooks, at convenient points, and I stopped at the first and admired the first of the five major cascades of Crabtree Falls. When I caught my breath, I took out the camera, snapped a few pictures, and continued my climb.

The trail has overlooks at the major cascades along the falls, and between the overlooks it winds around the mountain for some distance, then switches back to gain altitude. At difficult rocky sections, steps have been installed to make the hike easier and less dangerous.

Signs are regularly posted warning hikers to stay on the trail and not to venture too close to the falls, where slick rocks make hiking treacherous. Over the years, twenty-two people have died from falls.

The hike to the top of the falls is about two miles and all uphill, but the view is worth the effort. A wooden platform straddles the falls, and the view of the valley below is spectacular. The platform is situated so that it is not visible from the overlooks below, so it does not mar the view.

From the top of the falls the trail cuts through a thicket of mountain laurel and levels off as it follows Crabtree Creek to Crabtree Meadows. A parking area and rest rooms are here, and I noticed that some idiot, too lazy to drive to the landfill, had deposited about a dozen bags of garbage next to the women's rest room.

I thought then of Mr. Crabtree. Had he still been here and had he caught the perpetrators, I'll bet he would have given them a sound thumping.

Crabtree Falls at a Glance

GETTING THERE

Crabtree Falls is on Route 56 in Nelson County about eight miles off the Blue Ridge Parkway. Route 56 intersects with the parkway near milepost 27, which is twenty-seven miles west of Waynesboro. A parking area is on the right, a few miles past the community of Montebello.

STAYING THERE

Accommodations are available in Waynesboro, and the Wintergreen Resort is just off the parkway near milepost 13. A campground is in Montebello. Contact the Nelson County Division of Tourism at 800-282-8223 or visit their Web site at www.nelsoncounty.com.

BEST TIME TO GO

The falls are most spectacular after a period of wet weather. Water level in Crabtree Creek is low in summer and early fall. Winter through spring is considered the peak viewing period.

BE SURE TO BRING

Hiking boots or sturdy walking shoes are a good idea, especially if you intend to do the entire six-mile round-trip hike. The route is not difficult, but loose rocks and exposed roots make footing unstable. Shoes with good ankle support can prevent injury. A round-trip hike will take at least three hours, so bring water and something to eat.

FOR SAFETY'S SAKE

Stay on the trail and resist the urge to get closer to the falls. Twenty-two hikers have died from falling on slick rocks. Overlooks have been constructed at all five of the major cascades of the falls. The trail can be slick and dangerous in winter when it is covered with ice.

Warblers at Wintergreen

Fall is the time for birding in the Blue Ridge

Some birds are seldom seen but frequently heard. A towhee was in a thicket off the trail, and its voice was clear and unmistakable. "What do you want Santa to bring you for Christmas?" I asked.

"To-whees," the bird replied.

My wife, Lynn, and I were in the mountains southwest of Charlottesville, where the Blue Ridge narrows and funnels thousands of migrating birds through these hills each spring and fall. A mountain resort here is best known for skiing and golf, but it also has some thirty miles of hiking trails and six thousand acres of undisturbed forest, making it ideal habitat for migrating birds and those of us who like to watch them.

It was cloudy on the mountain, with a thick haze lying low in the valley. The air was still and heavy, so quiet you could hear your heart beat. The towhee's call was so clear and emphatic it was startling.

While towhees are year-round residents here, we were looking for smaller birds that would just be passing through this time of year—warblers, thrushes, tanagers—birds that travel to the northern United States and Canada each spring to raise a clutch of young and then return to winter homes in the tropics each fall.

We spotted our first in an oak tree not far off the trail. It was skittering nervously through the branches, apparently searching for small insects. Its small size and narrow bill made us think "warbler," but it was not until it fanned its tail, showing bold patches of yellow, that we recognized it as an American redstart.

The redstart is a fairly common warbler and one of the most striking. The yellow patches indicated that this was either a female or a young male. In mature males, those yellow patches become a deep salmon color, contrasting nicely with a rich black head, back, and breast.

The redstart was the first of numerous birds we saw, not all of which we could identify. Identifying warblers in the fall is much more difficult than in the spring for several reasons. In spring, male birds are dressed up in their breeding plumage, making identification much easier than in the fall, when the palette leans toward earth tones. And the birds are much more vocal in spring, singing to attract mates or to establish territory, so identifying birds by their song is much less likely in the fall.

But the forest was alive with birds, most of them migrants, most of them in what amounted to a feeding frenzy, fueling a migration that would take weeks and cover thousands of miles.

The forested slopes of the Blue Ridge are a migratory corridor for birds, something of an Interstate 81 for warblers and hawks intent on spending the winter in the mild climate of the tropics, where food abounds.

"The mountain here is really good for watching the fall migration, because the Blue Ridge narrows down here," says Doug Coleman, executive director of the Wintergreen Nature Foundation, a nonprofit organization based at the resort. "Hawk-watching is especially good along the ridges because the birds ride the wind currents. When the prevailing wind is from the northwest the birds tack like sailboats down the mountain range. But when the wind stops they ride the thermals, circling higher and higher, finally peeling off and gliding southward for miles until they find the next thermal."

Coleman said the fall hawk migration is weather-driven, with the peak coming usually in mid- to late September. "When we get a change in the weather and that northwest wind, it's not uncommon to see broadwing hawks by the hundreds," said Coleman.

The Wintergreen Nature Foundation and the Virginia Museum of Natural History host a Natural History Retreat Weekend each September at the resort, hoping to time the event with the peak of the bird migration. "The retreat began a number of years ago as a birding weekend, and we've expanded it to cover everything from butterflies to geology, but we still try to schedule it at the peak of the fall migration," Coleman said. "There's just something about standing here on this mountain and watching hundreds of hawks circle and glide and move on southward down the Blue Ridge. It gives you a new appreciation for how special this place is."

Wintergreen at a Glance

GETTING THERE

The Blue Ridge narrows south of Waynesboro, and the trails and overlooks along the parkway are good places to spot migrating songbirds and hawks. The parkway entrance is off I-64 at the Waynesboro exit.

WINTERGREEN NATURE FOUNDATION

The foundation is a nonprofit organization with headquarters at the resort. The foundation maintains hiking trails and holds regular natural history programs to promote understanding of the natural environment of the Blue Ridge. A Natural History Retreat Weekend is held each September in cooperation with the Virginia Museum of Natural History. Wildflower workshops are held in May. For information on these and other events call 434-325-7451.

HAWK-WATCHING

Hawks can be seen at many of the scenic stops along the Blue Ridge Parkway. Hawk-watching is best when the wind is from the northwest, although hawks can be seen climbing on thermals, which are columns of rising warm air created by the sun's heating of areas such as plowed fields or parking lots. Good-quality binoculars or a spotting scope are helpful in observing birds. A field guide is indispensable for identification.

WARBLER-WATCHING
The migration of songbirds such as warblers, thrushes, and tanagers begins in late August and continues through October, with the greatest variety of birds coming during September. Woodland trails at Wintergreen and along the Blue Ridge Parkway are good places to spot these migrants. Bring binoculars and a good field guide to birds.

OTHER FALL MIGRANTS
Doug Coleman of the Wintergreen Nature Foundation says fall is the ideal time to see migrating monarch butterflies, which are on their way to Central America. Migrating dragonflies can also be seen along the ridges.

Sherando Lake

*Springtime awakens in
the Blue Ridge*

I have difficulty thinking of a rock as a nice place for a nap, but I was tired and this one looked particularly inviting. It was large and flat, washed in sunlight, and when I lay back on it I could feel its warmth through my shirt.

I closed my eyes and listened. A cold front was approaching, and a stiff breeze whipped through the treetops. Leaf buds were on the trees, but they had not yet opened. Brown oak leaves still clung to some lower limbs, and I could hear them rattle in the wind. Below where I lay, to my right, a small stream swirled over rocks and emptied into Sherando Lake. I could hear the water tumble. And then I heard a pine warbler singing, a musical trill so loud and clear it startled me, like the ringing of a phone when I'm on the edge of sleep.

The previous evening I had visited Garvey and Deane Winegar of Waynesboro, authors of the *Highroad Guide to the Virginia Mountains*. We were talking about the value of using all our senses when experiencing the outdoors, not simply enjoying the visual beauty of a particular place, and Deane mentioned that she can identify maple trees by the sound the leaves make when they are jostled by the breeze.

So when I began my hike at Sherando, I decided to slow down and not simply enjoy the view, but to listen to the mountain. I often find it difficult being a good listener. Sometimes I'm so overwhelmed by the visual beauty of a place I ignore its more subtle values. Or I'm in too much of a hurry to truly listen. Or I'm immersed in a conversation with a hiking companion.

Sometimes it's necessary to go alone, which I did on this particular trip. I hadn't been in the mountains all winter, and I needed a mountain fix. So I got myself out to the Blue Ridge.

While the Virginia coast is in my blood, I love going to the mountains, and I don't do so nearly enough. After all, Tidewater is enticingly close. You can have breakfast at home, pack the car, and have a picnic lunch at noon on a trail in the Blue Ridge. If traffic is moving on I-64, you can be in Waynesboro in three or four hours, and from there head either south on the Blue Ridge Parkway or north on the Skyline Drive, quickly gaining access to miles of footpaths in the George Washington National Forest or Shenandoah National Park.

I began my trip at Humpback Rock, near the visitor center at milepost 5 on the parkway. The site offers a great view of the valley, and there is an old farmstead that provides a glimpse of what life might have been like for settlers who accepted government land grants in exchange for populating the western part of the state.

I then drove south on the parkway, turned right, and headed into the valley, and, at the suggestion of Garvey and Deane Winegar, visited Sherando Lake. The Sherando Lake Recreation Area was created in 1936 by the Civilian Conservation Corps, and in the summer it is a popular swimming, fishing, and camping area. But when I visited recently, the campgrounds were not yet open for the season, and only a few hardy fishermen were trying their luck on the shoreline.

A hiking trail circles the twenty-four-acre lake, providing access for fishermen and an easy walk for hikers. For those inclined toward a more strenuous hike, the Cliff Trail on the eastern side of the lake will provide a bit of an aerobic workout and reward you with a terrific view.

The temperature was in the lower sixties when I hiked the trail, but I worked up a sweat by the time I reached the summit along the ridge. My flatlander legs had that familiar burning sensation I get when I walk in the hills after a long layoff. The view, though, was worth the effort.

On my left was a steep valley, and beyond it the ridge where the parkway runs. On my right was Sherando Lake, glistening in the sunlight in the valley below. The trail runs along the ridge the entire length of the lake, providing not only a panoramic view but also a good chance to see wildlife. I spotted a group of deer in the eastern valley; and migrating warblers could be seen, or heard, in the tree-tops.

In early spring, the trail was still showing signs of winter. Ice storms and winds had buffeted the forest, downing some trees, snapping the tops out of others. Some lay across the trail, necessitating a short detour.

The flat rock I used for my rest stop was on the western side of the trail, overlooking the lake. It was in a perfect location, as if someone had used a giant crane to lower it into position.

I lay back, absorbing the warmth of the sun held in the rock. I looked up, and the tops of the bare trees waved in the wind. A front was approaching from the west, and gray clouds were gathering. It was one of those yin-yang days—something of hot, something of cold. The sun's warmth, and that of the rock, promised spring. But in the bite of the wind and in the gray clouds, something of winter remained.

Sherando Lake at a Glance

GETTING THERE
Sherando Lake is south of Waynesboro in Augusta County. Take exit 96 from I-64 and go two miles south on Route 624 to Lyndhurst. Bear left onto Route 664 and continue eight miles to the Sherando Lake entrance on the right.

WHAT TO DO
Hiking, swimming, fishing, boating (no motors), bird-watching, picnicking, wildflower watching. Interpretive programs are available. Contact the visitor center for schedule.

CAMPING

The camping areas are open from April 1 through October 31. There are three campground loops with a total of sixty-five sites, plus a group-camping area for 125 people. Contact them for information on reservations and fees.

FOR MORE INFORMATION

Contact the Glenwood and Pedlar Ranger District, P.O. Box 10, Natural Bridge, VA 24579. Phone 540-291-2188.

The Chessie Trail

This seven-mile footpath links Lexington and Buena Vista

A forest smells best when a summer rain falls early in the morning and then the sun comes out and gets things cooking. It's a wonderful aroma, rich and a bit pungent, like nothing that comes from a kitchen.

I was in Lexington not long ago and decided to hike the Chessie Nature Trail, a seven-mile footpath that runs along the Maury River to Buena Vista. It was early morning, and a warm rain had fallen, leaving puddles in the trail and turning the forest into a steaming factory of photosynthesis. Leaves seemed to grow as I watched them; insects danced nervously from flower to flower as if they had been too long at the morning coffee.

The Chessie Nature Trail is owned by the VMI Foundation and runs along an old C&O Railroad right-of-way. The railroad ceased operations here in 1969 after Hurricane Camille flooded the Maury River and wiped out the East Lexington trestles and much of the roadbed. In 1979 the VMI Foundation accepted ownership and agreed to manage the right-of-way as a public hiking path.

The national rails-to-trails system is one of America's great ideas. Today, more than a thousand trails cover ten thousand miles across the country. In Virginia, some of our most spectacular hiking and biking trails are former roadbeds. The Virginia Creeper Trail runs thirty-four miles from Whitetop to Abingdon. The New River Trail spans more than fifty miles between Galax and Pulaski. The Chessie is more modest in length, but, like the Creeper and the New River, it runs alongside a whitewater river that makes a hike something out of the ordinary.

The trail is not easy to find for out-of-town visitors unfamiliar with Lexington. It begins north of downtown Lexington just off Route 631, which intersects with U.S. Route 11 at the bridge over the Maury. I turned east on Route 631 but found that the parking area where the trailhead was supposed to be had been chained off.

A Pure Oil dealership was nearby, so I stopped and asked the folks there. They pointed out the trail entrance and kindly offered to let me park in the shade behind their office.

And so I was off toward Buena Vista, the sounds of Route 11 traffic fading away behind me. To my right was the Maury River, low and a bit languid, and on the opposite side of the path was a steep slope covered in green. Phoebes perched on oak limbs and bobbed their tails; I could hear towhees foraging and calling in the undergrowth.

Soon after entering the trail I crossed VMI Island, which at one time was an important approach to the city of Lexington. You crossed VMI Island when entering from the north, first by ford, and from 1835 until 1935 by a covered wooden bridge. Stone abutments of the old bridge are still visible on both sides of the river.

The river itself was an important vehicle of commerce. Sturdy wooden bateaux, designed for rough river travel, transported freight downstream. Later, Lexington would be linked to Richmond via the James River and Kanawha Canal system, and at that time the island was lined with warehouses and wharves for the mule-drawn barges.

The birth of the Chessie Trail came in 1880 when another avenue of commerce, the railroad, came to town and eventually replaced the slower canal system as Lexington's transportation route to the east. So the path that I walked, once a towpath, then a railroad, had now come full circle. As in the days when the American Indians roamed these hills, transportation was by foot.

The Maury River, which carved the spectacular Goshen Pass northwest of Lexington, is tamer here. It has a reputation as a fine fishing river, and when I stopped for lunch at the ruins of an old lock and dam, I decided to make it a point to come back later with the fly rod.

At Reid's lock and dam, mules and horses that had pulled barges from VMI Island along the towpath toward Buena Vista were ferried across the river, where they resumed their journey on the opposite bank.

Today the site provides a good break from the trail. A wide stone shelf is perfect for lying back in the sun, resting the legs, and having a bite to eat before heading on.

I took off my hiking boots and socks, walked down to the water, and waded in. It was surprisingly cool, carrying with it the reminders of colder water and higher elevations.

And in a still pool I saw the quick wake of a fish, probably a small-mouth bass. I was near the halfway point of the trail, near the Stuartsburg Road crossing, where there is a small parking area. The fly rod and tackle box were in the trunk of the car back at the Pure dealership, but I figured I could return in plenty of time to drive back to the crossing and get in a few hours' fishing in the afternoon.

They call the Chessie Trail a "multiple use" trail, and I hoped to prove them right. Already I had learned a little history, had gotten up close with nature, and had enjoyed a spectacular landscape. To end the day with a fly rod bent under the weight of a smallmouth bass seemed entirely proper.

The Chessie Trail at a Glance

GETTING THERE

The Chessie Nature Trail begins in Lexington along Route 631 on the Maury River. It follows the river seven miles to Buena Vista, where there is access off Route 60 on Stuartsburg Road. There also is access midway on Stuartsburg Road at the confluence of the Maury and the South Rivers. A footbridge constructed on an old railroad trestle provides a great view here.

STAYING THERE

Motels and restaurants are numerous in Lexington and Buena Vista, and Lexington has many historic sites as well as Virginia Military Institute and Washington and Lee University. Contact the Lexington Visitors Center, 106 East Washington Street, Lexington, VA 24450. Phone 540-463-3777.

FOR TRAIL INFORMATION

A brochure on the trail is available at the visitors' center, and a "Field Guide to the Chessie Nature Trail" was published by the Rockbridge Area Conservation Council in 1988. It's available in local bookstores. Note that the trail is open to hikers only. Bicycles and other vehicles are not allowed.

Doubtlessly Douthat

Douthat State Park in the off season offers peace and quiet with a scenic backdrop

So you want to get away from it all, do you? Want some peace? Want some quiet? Ready for a little mountain music? Douthat State Park in the off season is just the ticket.

Douthat is in the Allegheny Mountains north of the town of Clifton Forge. In the summer, the lake there is dotted with little aluminum johnboats, the beach is littered with screaming kiddies, and the pungent aroma of sunscreen fills the mountain air.

But in fall and winter, the kiddies are back in school, and the johnboats are turned upside down and strapped to lakeside racks. The sunscreen has been lost and will have to be replaced next May.

If you visit Douthat in the off season, especially midweek, it's like having your own personal state park. The park has forty miles of hiking trails, and when I visited I spent a day on them without seeing another hiker. A few people were fishing along the lakeshore, but even they seemed to be doing it halfheartedly, sitting in lawn chairs, wrapped in sweaters, dozing in the sun.

Douthat State Park is nearly in West Virginia, so if you live in eastern Virginia it's not the closest mountain getaway, but getting there is part of the fun. I left the interstate in Waynesboro and took U.S. Route 340 to U.S. Route 11, heading toward Lexington. Just east of town I turned right onto Route 39, which is designated a Virginia Byway, and for good reason.

The two-lane road twists and turns like a roller coaster through the George Washington National Forest. It slices its way through Goshen Pass, then continues northwestward to West Virginia, offering side trips along the way to Warm Springs and Hot Springs, home of the famous Homestead resort.

I hung a left in Millboro Springs on Route 629 and made my way to Douthat via another twisting roadway, with national forest on both sides. You can get to Douthat quicker by taking Interstate 64 to Clifton Forge and then taking exit 27 (Route 629) to the park. But the drive through Goshen Pass and the George Washington National Forest is certainly more enjoyable than jockeying for position with the big rigs on the interstate.

Douthat is one of Virginia's older state parks. It was built during the Civilian Conservation Corps days of the 1930s and is listed on the National Register of Historic Places for the role its design played in the development of parks nationwide.

Central to the park is a fifty-acre lake that was created by building a spillway on Wilson Creek. The lake has a sandy beach, boat rentals (in season), and both it and Wilson Creek are stocked with trout. Trails cover the circumference of the lake, making an easy and scenic hike of about two miles.

For those in search of a more challenging hike, Douthat offers twenty-four trails totaling some forty miles. Several include difficult sections along mountain ridges. A trail guide is available at the visitor center, and it includes not only a trail map but a table that classifies the trails according to degree of difficulty.

Among the easier walks, for example, would be the YCC Trail and Heron Run Trail, which circle Douthat Lake. Wilson Creek and Buck Lick Trails are listed as moderate, and the Tuscarora Overlook Trail and Brushy Hollow Trail are deemed difficult and recommended for experienced mountain hikers. Most of the trails are open to mountain bikes as well as pedestrians.

While Douthat during the off season is a great escape for a day hike, it also is a bargain for those who need a more prolonged period of peace and quiet. You can rent a one-bedroom cabin cheaply ($333 a week when I visited) during the off season. Some of the cabins are closed for the winter, but the park usually keeps a few open year-round.

I believe it was the poet Wordsworth who wrote, "The world is too much with us."

When the world is too much with me, I can think of no better place to escape it than Douthat State Park.

Douthat State Park at a Glance

GETTING THERE

I prefer the backdoor approach to Douthat State Park, taking scenic Route 39 west from Lexington. Turn onto Route 629 at Millboro Springs and follow it to the park. A faster alternative would be to take I-64 to Clifton Forge, then take exit 27 and follow Route 629 four miles to the park.

STAYING THERE

Cabins and camping facilities are available at the park. Many of the cabins close in December, but the park keeps nine open year-round. They are available on a first-come basis. Call 800-933-PARK or 804-225-3867 for reservations and information. Motels are available in nearby Clifton Forge and Covington, as are restaurants, laundromats, grocery stores, and pharmacies.

BE SURE TO BRING

Sturdy hiking boots are recommended for advanced trails. The altitude of the park is around three thousand feet, so temperatures will be cooler than in the lower elevations. Dress accordingly. Weather conditions can also change rapidly in late fall and winter. Many of the amenities such as the restaurant and snack bar are closed in winter, so bring food, drink, and other necessities.

WANT TO FISH?

A Virginia freshwater fishing license is required for fishing in Douthat Lake and Wilson Creek. Regulations covering fishing at Douthat are posted throughout the park and are listed in the Department of Game and Inland Fisheries Freshwater Fishing Guide.

The Civilian
Conservation Corps

*Those of us who like to hike are indebted
to the men who built our first parks*

From cabin 12, Buck Hollow Trail runs up the mountain and connects with Brushy Hollow Trail, which twists along the summit of Beards Mountain for nearly four miles. But if you don't feel like hiking, you can go downhill from cabin 12, rent a canoe, and fish for rainbow trout in Douthat Lake. If you're feeling completely lazy and worthless, you can sit on the front porch and strum the guitar and listen to the cicadas rub their legs together.

Our family spent a week in a cabin at Douthat State Park, a trip that made me realize how much those of us who enjoy the outdoors owe to a group of people who lived and worked in this park seventy years ago. The men of the Civilian Conservation Corps (CCC) built those trails on Beards Mountain. They built the stone dam on Wilson Creek that created Douthat Lake. They even built the log cabin that my wife and son and I called home for seven days.

The CCC was born of the Depression. In March 1933 more than 13 million people were unemployed in the United States. President Franklin D. Roosevelt, only two days after his inauguration, created the CCC, intending to put five hundred thousand unemployed youths to work in forests and parks around the country.

The CCC lasted for nine years and employed more than 3 million men. They built more than forty thousand bridges, planted 2 billion trees, restored historic structures, and improved roadways and shorelines.

Virginia opened its first six state parks in June 1936, thanks to the young men of the CCC who built trails, lakes, lodges, campgrounds, roads, and offices. Those of us who enjoy hiking, fishing, camping, and other outdoor activities benefit from the work of CCC volunteers even today.

Cabin 12 at Douthat is made of logs cut and shaped by the CCC men. The large stone fireplace was made by CCC masons. Most of the metal door latches were made in the CCC blacksmith shop. The hinges on the bedroom doors are made of wood, by CCC craftsmen.

Considering that the cabin was built some sixty-five years ago and has been lived in by thousands of weekly guests, the fact that these details remain intact is testimony to the workmanship of the CCC men. Cabin 12 has had its share of modern renovations; the plumbing is modern, and the summer humidity is controlled by a heat pump, but there still is evidence of older days. On the front porch, where an oil lantern once lighted the entryway, a black plume of soot rises along the wall where the lantern hung.

The CCC workers didn't live in the cabins they built. Those were for guests. They lived instead in camps, in military-style barracks, and they ate in mess halls. Most, however, seemed to enjoy the life, at least according to interviews given years after the CCC experience. The food was good, and the work was hard but rewarding. The young men were learning skills that they could employ in the workplace later in life.

CCC men were between the ages of eighteen and twenty-five, unmarried and unemployed. They came from families on relief, and twenty-five dollars of their thirty-dollar monthly wage was sent back home. Volunteers enlisted for six-month commitments, with a maximum term of service of two years.

A typical day in the life of a CCC enlistee began with 6:00 A.M. reveille, breakfast, barracks inspection, and then work. They returned to the barracks at 5:00 P.M., had dinner at 6:00 P.M. and then classes and recreational activities until 9:00 P.M., when the lights went out.

The CCC men ate well. A menu from the period lists oatmeal, hotcakes, bacon, fruit, and coffee for breakfast. Lunch was roast beef, mashed potatoes, green beans, cole slaw, bread, and chocolate pudding. Dinner was beef stew, baked potatoes, peas, tomatoes, bread, and iced tea.

When Virginia simultaneously opened six state parks in 1936, much of the credit went to the young men of the CCC. The original state parks are Douthat, Westmoreland, Hungry Mother, Fairy Stone, Staunton River, and Seashore (now First Landing) in Virginia Beach. All of these have seen major improvements over the years, with the addition of RV camping sites, swimming pools, interpretive centers, and mountain biking trails. But the mission of the parks remains as it was in 1936, to provide Virginia residents and visitors with a place to escape the urban grind and enjoy the outdoors.

The original mission of the CCC was to reforest federal land that had been logged. But the partnership that later developed with states gave rise to a park system enjoyed by millions generations later. The CCC may have been born of the Depression, but its legacy has left all of us who enjoy the outdoors a little bit richer.

The Civilian Conservation Corps at a Glance

THE CCC MUSEUM

A look at life in the Civilian Conservation Corps is provided by the CCC Museum at Pocahontas State Park near Chester, south of Richmond. The CCC helped develop the park that would become Pocahontas. Fittingly, the museum is in a renovated lodge originally constructed by CCC workers.

Sweet Land
of Goshen

*Trout and more on
the Maury River*

Trout live in only the finest neighborhoods. If you're looking for trout, go to a tumbling stream in a mountain forest—the farther from civilization, the better. Find a stream that rolls over boulders and snakes its way around slick rocks, forming quiet pools to contrast with rushing whitewater. Find a landscape that could have been taken from a painting, and you'll find trout.

I was standing on a suspension bridge halfway across the Maury River, looking at the cold water rushing by thirty feet below. The bridge swayed, and I braced myself against the railing and searched the quiet pools for trout. Of course, I could see none. They were far too accomplished at the art of camouflage to be seen at thirty feet by a mere human.

Still, it was nice to look into those pools and contemplate movement, a quick flash of shadow that would mean fish.

West of Lexington, the Maury River grinds its way through a crease between Little North and Hogback Mountains called Goshen Pass. It is prime real estate for trout—cold, tumbling water framed in a landscape that makes fishing a wonderful sport, regardless of whether you come home with fish.

Trout are creatures of dignity. You won't find them in turbid water that smells funny in August or in places where unwanted appliances are dumped from bridges. Trout prefer clear water that is cold and well-oxygenated from tumbling over rocks. They prefer rolling land where hemlocks, rhododendron, and mountain laurel grow.

And this business of fishing for trout, especially with fly rod, is transcendental, becoming something much larger than an attempt to put a fish into a creel. In literature, trout-fishing is frequently a metaphor for life. In Hemingway's *Big Two-Hearted River,* trout-fishing is a ritual of healing and recovery. Trout-fishing is the thread that binds father and sons in Norman MacLean's *A River Runs through It.*

As I stood on the swaying footbridge, I watched two women fishing on the riverbank below me. I doubt they were aware of the metaphorical significance of what they were up to. They were using spinning rods and worms and were clearly enjoying themselves. I left the bridge and stopped to say hello.

Their baits moved swiftly in the current. It was a cool morning in late fall, and a few leaves still clung to the hardwoods, ragged but holding color. The women cast like experts, locating the dark pools where a trout might lie in ambush.

Suddenly a trout hit, and the line became taut. The woman reeled quickly and backed away from the water. Soon the fish was in the shallows, gleaming like a spotted jewel, its gill covers pulsing. It was a small fish but a beautiful one. The women laughed and admired it for a long time before placing it into the creel. It was their first of the day.

Fishing the Maury River at Goshen Pass is a situation in which the landscape probably overrules the sport. We don't come here for fish; we come here for the experience of fishing in one of Virginia's most dramatic landscapes.

Route 39 intersects with U.S. Route 11 just north of Lexington. For the first few miles, Route 39 runs through rolling suburbia, with the huge Virginia Horse Center complex on the left. But soon the landscape becomes wilder, the road becomes twisty, and the Maury River runs alongside. It passes through Cedar Grove, Rockbridge Baths, and then through the pass called Goshen, which is a few miles east of the town called Goshen.

The cliffs here are tall and steep, and most of the time the river is somewhat riled. It snakes around huge boulders and can be heard even when it is not seen. From a scenic pullover on Route 39, Goshen Pass appears to have been transplanted from the far west. It is a dramatic and emphatic landscape, geology flexing its muscles.

Farther along Route 39 the state maintains a wayside on the right, with a shelter, rest rooms, and picnic tables. The river is easily accessible here, and it's where most people begin their fishing trips.

If fishing is not a priority, the Goshen area has miles of access roads and hiking trails. The state's largest Wildlife Management Area (WMA), Goshen-Little North Mountain, straddles the Maury here and totals more than thirty-three thousand acres. The WMA is managed for hunting, fishing, and other outdoor activities. North of the WMA is George Washington National Forest, so there is plenty of public land here for exploring.

The Maury River was named in honor of Matthew Fontaine Maury, who is considered the father of oceanography. Maury was born in 1806 in Spotsylvania County and, after a distinguished naval career, became a pioneer in the study of ocean currents. He later taught physics at VMI in Lexington.

This body of water that bears his name is anything but oceanic; when the river is running low, its depth can be measured in inches. But it is a fitting tribute to a man who spent his life studying moving water. And I'll bet he was a trout fisherman.

Goshen at a Glance

GETTING THERE

Goshen Pass is on Route 39 about twelve miles north of Lexington in Rockbridge County. Route 39 intersects with U.S. Route 11 about a mile east of Lexington. Several scenic overlooks are located along

the roadway, and there is a picnic area along the river. A suspension
bridge just beyond the picnic area provides access to both sides of
the Maury River.

STAYING THERE

Numerous hotels, motels, and bed-and-breakfast establishments
are in the Lexington and Buena Vista area. Contact the Lexington-
Rockbridge County Visitors Center at 540-463-3777 or the Buena
Vista Regional Visitor Center at 540-261-2880.

ON THE RIVER

Trout-fishing in the Maury River is of the "put-and-take" variety,
meaning the stream is stocked regularly by the Virginia Department
of Game and Inland Fisheries (DGIF). A Virginia freshwater fishing
license is required as well as a trout stamp in stocked areas, which are
well-posted. Contact the DGIF for information on fishing the
Maury and for a guide to the Goshen–Little North Mountain WMA.
The phone number is 804-367-1000. When the river is running high
and navigable, it is popular with whitewater paddlers and rafters.

It's Called Fishing,
Not Catching

*The James River Wildlife Management Area
offers a break from the daily grind*

When I'm traveling, I often take along some fishing tackle. It's a modest little arsenal of equipment but one that will serve should I feel the need to leave the world behind for a half-day to search for bass or trout.

I have a spinning reel mounted on a six-foot, medium-light-action rod. The reel is spooled with six-pound test line, and I have in a small plastic box about a dozen lures: spinner baits, plastic grubs, worms, and the like.

Should I find myself with a few free hours, I'll seek out a body of water with public access and go fishing. I seldom catch fish, but the act of fishing instantly erases the stress of travel; it gets me off the highway and down some back road the rest of the world doesn't know about.

In most cases, when I feel the need to fish, I'll seek out one of Virginia's Wildlife Management Areas, or WMAs. These are publicly owned tracts of land, most of which were purchased by the state with proceeds from hunting, fishing, and trapping licenses, and with taxes paid on equipment purchased for those sports.

Virginia's WMAs are probably the most overlooked and under-appreciated public resources in the state. There are twenty-nine of them, with a total of 180,000 acres, and they cover Virginia from corner to corner, from Mockhorn Island on the Eastern Shore to Hidden Valley in Washington County.

The WMAs are administered by the Department of Game and Inland Fisheries (DGIF), and the management techniques tend to emphasize game animals. So the primary constituencies are Virginia hunters, and, to a lesser extent, fishermen.

But hunting seasons are relatively short, and these 180,000 acres are open year-round for all of us to enjoy, regardless of whether we purchased hunting and fishing licenses to help defray the costs. WMAs are open to bicycling, hiking, birding, horseback-riding, boating, and a number of other activities, in addition to hunting and fishing.

While land management is geared toward game species, WMAs obviously benefit wildlife in general. Those sunflowers planted to attract doves might also nourish indigo buntings, goldfinches, and red-winged blackbirds. The unmowed meadows, hedgerows, and brush piles will provide shelter for migrating warblers, blue grosbeaks, and other songbirds as well as for rabbits and quail.

Management of the twenty-nine WMAs makes the DGIF the administrator of more public land than any other state agency, including the Department of Forestry and the Division of State Parks.

Indeed, Virginia's WMAs could be thought of as state parks without the bells and whistles, and without the fee schedule posted at the entrance gate. While many of our state parks have improvements such as rental cabins, swimming pools, restaurants, and camper hookups, WMAs tend to be spartan. Camping is allowed, but it is of the "primitive" variety. And if you want a tuna sandwich for lunch, you'd better bring it with you. Wildlife gets the emphasis here.

State WMAs cover a wide variety of terrain, and they vary greatly in size. Goshen–Little North Mountain in Augusta County is mountainous, and at nearly thirty-four thousand acres, is the state's largest WMA. Most range from a thousand to five thousand acres.

Not long ago I was in Nelson County with a few hours to spare one afternoon. It was one of those early winter days that refuses to relinquish its grip on fall. I drove from Lovingston on Route 29 to Shipman and took Route 56 down to the James River, where the state maintains a 1,213-acre WMA named for Virginia's most famous river.

The James is wide and languid here, flowing quietly under overhanging trees. An old riverfront estate once stretched along the banks, and the cemetery still provides a human link to this area now managed for wildlife.

I took my fishing rod and lures from the car and walked down to the bank of the river, feeling like Huck Finn stealing away for an afternoon alone with the water. I tied on a Mepps spinner and cast it into the current, watching it sink under dead leaves.

I didn't much expect to catch a fish, and it really wasn't what I was there for. Perhaps that's why I pack that fishing rod when I travel. It has nothing to do with catching fish but everything to do with fishing.

Wildlife Management Areas at a Glance

WANT TO KNOW MORE?

The Department of Game and Inland Fisheries has published a 68-page directory of the twenty-nine state Wildlife Management Areas. It is available free of charge from DGIF offices. A more comprehensive guide is Bob Gooch's *Enjoying Virginia's Outdoors: A Guide to Wildlife Management Areas,* published by the University of Virginia Press in Charlottesville. The 238-page guide sells for $18.95 and can be purchased at local bookstores or directly from the university press. The e-mail address is upressva@virginia.edu.

IF YOU GO

State WMAs are purchased and managed by the proceeds from sales of hunting, fishing, and trapping licenses, so most are managed with those activities in mind. The best time to participate in other activities is when hunting is out of season or on Sundays during the season. If you do enter a WMA during the season, wear blaze orange for safety.

BUY A TICKET

Even if you don't hunt or fish, you could help the state manage and enlarge our WMAs by purchasing hunting and fishing licenses. Consider it the price of admission to 180,000 acres of Virginia open land.

Southwest
Virginia

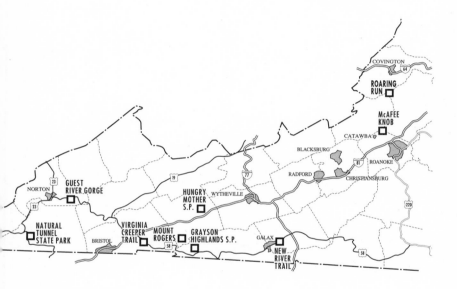

COVINGTON

ROARING
RUN

McAFEE
KNOB

CATAWBA

BLACKSBURG

ROANOKE

RADFORD

CHRISTIANSBURG

GUEST
RIVER GORGE

NORTON

HUNGRY
MOTHER
S.P.

WYTHEVILLE

NATURAL
TUNNEL
STATE PARK

VIRGINIA
CREEPER
TRAIL

MOUNT
ROGERS

GRAYSON
HIGHLANDS S.P.

GALAX

NEW
RIVER
TRAIL

BRISTOL

Bass and Whitewater

*Searching for smallmouth bass
on the upper James River*

A set of rapids was fast approaching, and we were heading for them stern-first. Just as our dory entered the first bit of whitewater, our guide leaned heavily on his right oar. The boat pirouetted, the high bow cut through the frothy water with ease, and within seconds we were back in the calm, ready to resume fishing.

We were on the upper James River west of the town of Buchanan, and fishing guide Blane Chocklett was coaching us in the finer points of catching smallmouth bass. Chocklett and his wife, Dru, run a fishing supply business in Roanoke, and he has been fishing for smallmouth in these waters since he was nine years old.

Lynn and I were spending a few days at a bed-and-breakfast in Catawba, and the proprietors, Bill and Katherine Cochran, introduced us to Chocklett, who offered to take us out in search of smallmouth.

The plan was to float about three miles of river near Springwood. "That section has some excellent structure with nice rapids," said Chocklett. "And it's definitely scenic."

"Scenic" could be putting it mildly. Lynn and I are used to fishing in the Chesapeake Bay, which in itself is scenic, but in something of an open and all-encompassing kind of way. Here on the James, mountains line the river like massive green walls, and the river hisses and tumbles its way over slick rocks.

Timber Ridge runs along the western horizon, and Purgatory Mountain is on the eastern side, so the river here is wild and remote, with few signs of civilization. We shared the river with only a few canoeists.

Chocklett's Hyde dory is an import from Idaho and something of a curiosity on the upper James. It is designed to be rowed stern-first, but its rockered bottom makes it very maneuverable. Chocklett easily pivots the boat when approaching rapids and takes them bow-first, with the sharply upturned foresection cutting through the whitewater.

When we pass a set of rapids, Chocklett sets anchor, and we cast toward the shoreline. He points out eddies where smallmouth may be lurking, and we cast lures there, Lynn and I using small plugs and spinner baits on our spinning rods, Chockett using a popping bug on his fly rod.

Action is slow on this particular Monday afternoon because the previous weekend had brought heavy boat traffic. "The fish are still spooked," says Chocklett. "This water is very shallow, and any kind of boat traffic shuts the fishing off. We normally catch and release about fifty bass on this particular float."

Chocklett needn't have apologized for the lack of fish. Lynn and I were taken with the landscape, the fast-moving river, and the thrill of riding the dory through a set of modest rapids, whitewater breaking against the bow. The dozen or so bass we caught and released simply added to the experience.

Chocklett, in his late twenties, is a young man living a dream. He began fly-fishing when he was nine, began tying his own flies a year later, and now is in the business of fishing. "I learned to fish from my grandfather and dad, and I liked it more than they did," he says. "I grew up in Botetourt County just a few minutes from the James, and we'd go fishing every weekend. I started guiding when I was in high school."

Chocklett attended Virginia Western Community College and

continued to guide and work in a fishing tackle shop in Roanoke, planning eventually to go to Virginia Tech. "I wasn't sure exactly what I wanted to do, but I knew I wanted to do something in fisheries," he says.

In 1996 he and Dru decided to postpone the academic approach to fisheries and see if they could build a business around the more pragmatic matters of catching fish and designing flies. In May of that year they opened their shop on Williamson Road in Roanoke and have been in business since.

"Dru convinced me that we were young, and if the business didn't work out I could always go back to school," he says. "But if I didn't try it, I'd always regret it."

The Chockletts have had no regrets so far.

The Williamson Road shop is filled with lures and flies of Chocklett's own design. There are first-quality fishing rods, reels, clothing, and all the other necessities you need for a day on the river. The dory, on its trailer, is parked in the lot outside.

Dru prefers the business world of fishing to the actual experience of being on the river, so she minds the shop while Chocklett rows clients through the riffles and eddies of the James.

When Chocklett isn't on the river, he is designing and tying flies that imitate prey species preferred by smallmouth bass. His talents at tying flies have not gone unnoticed. He submitted some of his designs to the Umpqua company of Eugene, Oregon, the largest fly supplier in the world. They liked his work, and now he is a contract tier for them.

After more than four years of having a successful business, the Chockletts feel that they made the right decision. The business is succeeding, and that means Chocklett gets to spend more time on the water.

The Upper James at a Glance

WANT TO KNOW MORE?

You can fish the upper James on your own or go with a guide. If you have little experience in fishing the area, a half-day trip with a knowledgeable guide would be a good investment. For information on guide services and other outdoor resources in the Roanoke, see the Roanoke Valley Convention and Visitors Bureau Web site at www .visitroanokeva.com. Another site with a wealth of information on hiking, biking, outdoor sports, and other things to do is www .roanoke.com.

BEST BAITS

If you fish on your own, ask at local tackle shops about best baits and lures for particular areas. For the upper James, Blane Chocklett recommends flies and lures that imitate prey species smallmouth feed on. These include dragonfly nymphs, various minnows, crayfish, and forage fish.

To McAfee Knob with Olen Waldrip

Nearing ninety, the mountain man keeps climbing

It was raining on Catawba Mountain. Olen Waldrip led us through a damp thicket of mountain laurel and onto a rocky outcropping called McAfee Knob. He lifted a walking stick overhead and gave a good Texas yell. Two years shy of his ninetieth birthday, Waldrip had just completed his 313th climb to this peak along the Appalachian Trail near Roanoke, a rocky hike of about seven miles.

As if on cue, the rain ended as we stood on the rocky ledge, so we took sandwiches from our packs and had lunch. Waldrip unsheathed a sturdy knife and carved a notch in a walking stick he had made from tulip poplar. He has a notch for each successful hike to McAfee Knob, which affords one of the most spectacular views along the 2,160-mile Maine-to-Georgia trail.

Waldrip calls himself a mountain man, and he looks the part. At eighty-eight, he is well-muscled, with broad shoulders and biceps that flex as he lifts and lowers his walking sticks. He wears cutoff blue jeans, a T-shirt, knee-length red socks, and a sturdy pair of hiking boots he bought at the Goodwill store in Roanoke for a dollar. On McAfee Knob he stands like a beacon in the mist, shouting aloud his joy at once again having reached the summit.

Lynn and I were introduced to Waldrip by Bill and Katherine Cochran of Catawba, who own a bed-and-breakfast business at the junction of the Appalachian Trail and the TransAmerica Bicycle Trail. We told the Cochrans we wanted to do a little hiking, and they suggested we accompany Waldrip on one of his hikes to McAfee Knob. "He enjoys the company," said Bill.

We met Waldrip for breakfast at the Cochrans' and explained that, as Tidewater natives, we define a hill as anything over forty feet above sea level. But Waldrip insisted he had a nice, easy trail for us, although the rain might make some of the rocky sections a mite slick.

I had a second cup of Katherine's cinnamon-flavored coffee and another helping of peach cobbler, buying time until either the rain ended or common sense would prevail and someone might suggest that the day was better suited for, say, a trip to the local shopping mall rather than a seven-mile climb up and down a mountain.

But Olen Waldrip is one of those perennially upbeat people who has never met a stranger and who considers rain only a temporary condition in what otherwise is a bright and sunny day. We began the hike wearing ponchos but stowed them in our packs long before the day was over as the sun gradually burned off the haze and illuminated the valley below us.

Waldrip is a retired Baptist minister whose deep voice and measured cadence reflect his years in the pulpit. On hike number 313 to McAfee Knob he approaches the trail with the enthusiasm of a child, pointing out wildflowers and interesting rock formations. He throws his head back and laughs loudly halfway through the hike when I suggest that he not be hesitant should he feel the need to, well, take a little rest break.

Waldrip grew up on a farm in Texas and early in life learned the value of hard work. "I didn't have any choice," he laughs. "Times were hard back then. When I was a child I was up every morning at 4:30 to work on the farm before going to school." Waldrip eventually went to college and then seminary, and he became pastor of a Texas congregation in May 1932.

He and his wife, Louise, a professor of English, moved to the Roanoke Valley upon retirement. Waldrip made his first climb to McAfee Knob in 1993 and later set a goal to make the hike enough times to equal the 2,160 miles of the Appalachian Trail, a feat he accomplished early in 2000.

Nearing ninety and with plenty of spare time, Waldrip still adheres to the daily schedule instilled in him as a Texas farm boy. He rises at 4:30 and begins an hour of exercise, including twelve trips up and down three flights of stairs while carrying dumbbells. He averages one trip per week to McAfee Knob.

"I missed two weeks last year because of snow," he says. "I came within a half-mile of the top but couldn't get to the Knob. I have a rule. If I don't eat my lunch on the Knob, I don't consider it a complete trip, and I don't cut a notch in my walking stick."

He retired one walking stick after three hundred notches and now is on his second. As he carved a notch during lunch on our recent hike, I noted that the stick was relatively new, with plenty of room for additional notches.

McAfee Knob at a Glance

GETTING THERE

McAfee Knob is accessible via the Appalachian Trail, but a fire road running near the trail provides easier walking, especially when conditions are less than ideal. It takes about six hours to hike to McAfee Knob and back to the parking area on Route 311. The trailhead is just outside the community of Catawba.

BE SURE TO BRING

Sturdy hiking boots are needed, and it's usually cooler at the higher elevations, so dress accordingly. A fanny pack or day pack is handy for carrying lunch, drinks, camera, and field guides.

Roaring Run

This waterfall near Roanoke is one of Virginia's most spectacular

Roaring Run was really roaring. Rain had begun Sunday morning and by noon Tuesday, when Mike Donahue and I neared the stream, it sounded like a freight train loaded with number-nine coal late for arrival in Roanoke.

We heard the stream before we saw it, a steady, determined growl, not rhythmic like ocean surf. We parked in a picnic area nearby, put on our rain jackets, and headed off on a trail that crosses the run and then parallels it for more than a mile.

It is a spectacular place, with hemlocks looming overhead, wild-flowers blooming on the forest floor, and what on most days is a classic little Virginia trout stream, a tame and picturesque cold-water brook stocked regularly with rainbow trout by the game department. But on the Tuesday when Donahue and I visited, the stream had become a river and was flexing its muscles, running fast and dirty, pushing deadfall hemlocks out of its path as it headed for Craig Creek and then the James River.

Roaring Run has Virginia's least known and most impressive waterfalls, which on our visit were putting on a July Fourth fireworks kind of show. The fall at the top of the trail is broad, and it drops perhaps sixty feet in an explosion of whitewater. Then the stream divides into several smaller falls that cut through the valley, sometimes pausing to relax in pools and at times snaking around boulders at impressive speed. From the top of the falls to the picnic area below, the drop is several hundred feet.

Few people outside the immediate area are familiar with Roaring Run. Ask a Tidewater resident to name a Virginia waterfall, and you'll probably get Crabtree Falls as the reply. Crabtree is in all the guidebooks, and it's just off the Blue Ridge Parkway near a large ski and golf resort, so it gets its fair share of visitors. Roaring Run is in the George Washington and Jefferson National Forests between Oriskany and Eagle Rock, neither of which is on many short lists of vacation getaways. As waterfalls go, though, I'd rate Roaring Run right up there with Mr. Crabtree, especially after two days of rain.

Mike Donahue is one of those exceptional field naturalists who is unspoiled by an excess of formal education. Until the mid-1990s he worked as a welder at a concrete block company in Roanoke, studying birds, wild plants, and butterflies in his spare time. Then the company shut down. Mike got his associate's degree and eventually got on with the U.S. Forest Service, and now he gets paid to study the wild things that once occupied his weekends and vacation time.

Unlike the doctoral candidates who emerge from universities with a deep but narrow angle of expertise, Donahue sees the big picture. He's an expert birder; he knows wild plants and butterflies and geology. Ask him a question about the stream dynamics of Roaring Run, and in his modest way he'll preface his reply with the phrase, "Well, I'm not a hydrologist, but . . . " and then he'll expertly answer your question.

When Donahue and I visited Roaring Run recently, he was wearing his botanist hat. Donahue and several other forest service biologists and local naturalists were preparing to lead a wildflower walk, and Donahue wanted to see what might be popping through the streamside soil. It was early in the spring, but Donahue quickly spotted signs that plant life was awakening after a winter of dormancy.

"Here's a trout lily," said Donahue. He kneeled and gently lifted a leaf. The plant was growing close to the ground, and the leaves had the shape of a trout as well as a vermiculated green color pattern similar to that of the fish. "This is one of our earliest wildflowers," added Donahue. "It's right on time."

Farther along the trail Donahue spotted wild ginger, which he said is pollinated by ground-dwelling beetles, and galax, the wildflower that gave its name to the southwest Virginia town famous for its fiddlers' convention. Donahue spotted foamflower growing alongside the trail and a small plant called rattlesnake plantain, whose naming I thought would be best not explored.

Donahue has been leading wildflower walks at Roaring Run for seven years, and he was expecting some fifty visitors. "This area is great for finding wildflowers," he said. "In a fairly limited area, more than 150 species of trees, shrubs, and plants have been recorded. Some are common to the area; others are a little more rare. The wildflower walk is especially good for people who are just learning wildflowers, because they get to spend the morning with an expert in an area that is rich with plants. A bonus is that the wildflower walk comes at the peak of the spring bird migration, so visitors not only get to see wildflowers in bloom, but they get to see a lot of warbler species as well."

And on the trail at Roaring Run, they also get to spend a day hiking along one of Virginia's least known, but most dramatic, waterfalls.

Roaring Run at a Glance

GETTING THERE

Roaring Run is between Roanoke and Clifton Forge in the George Washington and Jefferson National Forest. Take I-64 to Clifton Forge. Take the Low Moor exit and take Route 616 to Rich Patch and turn left onto Route 621. The Roaring Run picnic area will be on the right at the bottom of the hill. From the Roanoke area, take Route 220 to Eagle Rock, turn left onto Route 615, then right onto Route 621. The picnic area will be one mile down on the left.

STAYING THERE

Closest accommodations are in Clifton Forge and Covington, or in Roanoke south of the site. Both are about a forty-five-minute drive.

Camping and cabins are available at Douthat State Park near Clifton Forge.

AND WHILE YOU'RE THERE

Roaring Run has more than wildflowers and birds. It is a historic site, with the remains of an iron furnace that predates the Civil War. The furnace is on the banks of the stream a short distance from the picnic area and parking lot. The furnace site is handicapped accessible. The stream also is stocked with rainbow trout, so bring the fly rod.

THE WILDFLOWER WALK

The forest service sponsors a wildflower walk in early May each year. There is no charge to participate. The hike is about a mile and a half and covers gentle terrain. Bring a camera, binoculars for birding, and field guides. You might bring a picnic lunch also. For more information, contact the James River Ranger District of the George Washington and Jefferson National Forests at 540-962-2214.

The New River Trail

*This could be Virginia's most
spectacular bike ride*

I had never ridden a bicycle
through a railroad tunnel before, and, as the sunshine gave way to
pitch-black rock, it occurred to me that this might not be one of the
smartest things I'd ever done. The trail curved to the left, and, as it
did so, all light from behind was cut off. I groped for my battery-
powered taillight, couldn't find it, but soon was relieved to see the
proverbial light at the end of the tunnel some distance ahead of us.

We were on the New River Trail in southwest Virginia, not far
from Galax, and the tunnel was a memento of the former owner and
builder of the trail, Norfolk and Western Railroad Company, whose
steam engines once carried thousands of tons of iron ore from these
mountains to factories in the east.

The railroad now is long gone, the tracks removed, and the only
danger of navigating a dark tunnel is the chance of meeting another
biker, which is slim, or of interrupting the snooze of a black bear,
which is really slim.

The railroad once chugged its way through these mountain
passes, over streams, and through tunnels. Steam whistles enlivened
mining communities such as Foster's Falls, Ivanhoe, and Fries. The
only sounds along the former railbed today are those made by

Mother Nature. A redtail hawk soars and screams, hoping to get the attention of a prey. A belted kingfisher dives into the shallows of the New River, comes up with a small fish, and then flies off to a dead-fall, where it whacks the fish on the head and then swallows it whole.

The Norfolk Southern Corporation abandoned the railroad line in 1986 and donated the right-of-way to the state, which immediately began converting the line to a rails-to-trails park. The first four miles of trail opened in May 1987, and by 1995 the trail had grown to forty miles. In 1999 the final two miles were opened, creating an uninterrupted greenway of fifty-seven miles linking Galax and Pulaski, including a 5.5-mile spur to the town of Fries.

New River Trail today is one of Virginia's most unusual state parks in that it is linear. It contains 765 acres, yet averages only 80 feet in width. It runs through Grayson, Carroll, Wythe, and Pulaski Counties, with the southern terminus at U.S. Route 58 in Galax and the northern on Route 99 in Pulaski. The trail is open to bicyclists, walkers, and horseback riders; motor vehicles are prohibited.

Given the layout of the trail, you can begin a hike or ride from either end or from somewhere in the middle. The park runs through some rural areas, however, and developed parking facilities are limited. The best places to begin are in Galax, Pulaski, and at Foster Falls, where the park headquarters is located. If you're riding a bike, you can either pedal out and back, or you can arrange to have a shuttle meet you and return you to your vehicle.

On a recent trip to New River Trail, Lynn, Tom, and I tried both approaches. We arrived at park headquarters in early afternoon on a Friday, unloaded the bikes, and headed north toward Pulaski, intending to ride some ten miles and then turn back. Park headquarters is near milepost 24, and we rode to Reed Junction, where Reed Island Creek joins the New River. It was a spectacular ride, with the river alongside the trail the entire way, sometimes cascading over rocks, at other times flowing silently and deep.

We spent Friday night in Galax and left Saturday morning from milepost 51.5 on Route 58. The southern end of the trail follows Chestnut Creek until it joins New River at mile 40. So for nearly the entire ride—for more than fifty miles—you are biking alongside moving water.

The New River is unique for two reasons. One, it is not new at all; it is said to be the second-oldest river in the world. And unlike most rivers in North America, it flows from south to north. So the river is narrower along the southern portions, with whitewater often in evidence, although the river widens at Byllesby and Buck dams. There is a nice waterfall on Chestnut Creek just before the creek joins the river, and the trail offers a spectacular view of Claytor Lake near the northern terminus.

The ride from Galax to Foster's Falls took about four hours, including a stop for a trailside lunch and numerous leg-stretching breaks to enjoy the scenery. The trail includes some thirty trestles and bridges, almost all of which beg you to stop and appreciate the view. Some are only a few dozen feet in length, crossing a modest brook, but others are substantial bridges. The Fries Junction bridge is 1,089 feet long and can be intimidating to those with a fear of heights.

One of the most picturesque sections of the trail covers the few miles south of Foster's Falls. Along one stretch, hardwood trees create a canopy over the trail for a distance of about a mile. The New tumbles over boulders only a few feet away.

Our Saturday ride ended at park headquarters at Foster's Falls, which is adjacent to the Shot Tower State Historical Park, where munitions were made for Civil War soldiers. A primitive campground, picnic facilities, and bike and canoe rentals are available there. The canoe livery also offers a shuttle service for those who bring bikes and need a return trip to their vehicle. A large brick building on the site, originally a mining company hotel and later the county orphanage, is slated for renovation and use as a bed-and-breakfast.

New River Trail, because it follows a former railroad right-of-way, has a very gentle grade, running slightly downhill from Galax to near Pulaski. The elevation is around twenty-four hundred feet at Galax, dropping about five hundred feet over the next forty miles. The trail surface is packed stone and cinders, mostly material left from railroad days.

It is an easy ride but probably best suited to hybrids or mountain bikes. Soft spots and occasional large stones can make the trail hazardous for narrow-tired road bikes. Lynn and I rode our hybrids, and even then she took a nasty spill when the front wheel got twisted in some loose cinders. During fall and winter, leaves can overlay the trail, making some sections slick. When we go back, we'll take mountain bikes.

Because the trail is shared by cyclists, hikers, and horseback riders, courtesy is called for, especially when you're on a bike. Cyclists should pull over when horseback riders approach, and they should let their presence be known to walkers before passing.

Many sections of the trail are remote, so bring food, drink, and minimum bike-repair gear, including a tube repair kit, tire levers, and Allen wrenches. Some minimum first-aid equipment is also a good idea, says Lynn. Water for cleaning road rash, some gauze, and a tube of antibacterial ointment would be a good starting point.

The New River Trail at a Glance

GETTING THERE

Galax is on U.S. Route 58 just west of Interstate 77. Pulaski is just off Interstate 81 at exit 94.

STAYING THERE

Numerous motel accommodations are available in Galax, Pulaski, and Wytheville. Primitive camping is allowed on the trail at Foster's Falls and at Cliffview on Chestnut Creek near Galax.

CALL FIRST

Some services, such as bike shuttle and rentals, are available on a seasonal basis, so call the park headquarters (540-699-6778) before visiting to determine availability.

Grayson Highlands

Standing at the summit of Virginia

As I stood on the rock outcropping and looked over the valley below, I was seized with the urge to do something no reasonably sane middle-aged man should ever do.

"The hillllls are alive, with the sound of muuuusic!" I sang.

That felt good. I don't come from a musical family, and that is something I have always regretted.

I was standing on a volcanic rock, the larger of a pair called Twin Pinnacles, and off in the distance was Mount Rogers, the tallest point in Virginia at 5,729 feet. Not far away was Whitetop Mountain, which is not exactly dwarfish. Down in the valley, the few visible houses looked like matchbox toys; cars could have been ants creeping along a little sugar trail.

I had gotten here by walking a 1.6-mile trail through ferns, hawthorns, and witch hazel, finally climbing layers of rock, and then emerging in the bright sunlight to what must be one of the most stunning views in Virginia.

You know it makes me wanna shout.

I was in Grayson County, which is almost in North Carolina but looks like it's in Canada. Trees grow here in these heady altitudes that usually are found much farther north. Even birds nest here that in the summer are supposed to be in New Brunswick or somewhere. If you look at the range maps in your field guide, you'll note that the summer range of many birds is mainly in Canada, but a little finger (colored yellow in my guide) dips down the Appalachians all the way to North Carolina.

That's because of climate, and in these parts climate is governed by altitude. For example, Abingdon is about fifty miles west of here and about thirty-five hundred feet closer to sea level. The climate, and the flora and fauna, are very different.

Perhaps that's also why many of us who live in the lower elevations like to migrate to the mountains during the muggy days of late summer and early fall. Like all creatures, our movements are governed by climate; we go where we are most comfortable.

Grayson County has a wealth of places such as this. I was in Grayson Highlands State Park, which borders the Mount Rogers recreation area, part of the Jefferson National Forest. So there are thousands of acres of public land open for wandering; and the Appalachian Trail, the famous Maine-to-Georgia footpath, runs through the middle of it.

Grayson Highlands State Park is on U.S. Route 58 near the community of Mouth of Wilson in Grayson County, a few miles west of Galax. The park offers the usual amenities such as camping and picnic facilities, but the trails are a major draw. In addition to the Appalachian Trail, there are a number of shorter hiking trails within the park boundaries that vary in distance and difficulty.

The Twin Pinnacles Trail, for example, begins behind the visitor center and climbs gently to the top of Haw Orchard Mountain. The loop trail covers 1.6 miles. Listening Rock Trail is an even 2 miles, Stampers Branch Trail is 1.7 miles, and Cabin Creek Trail is 1.9 miles. All the trails offer spectacular views, from panoramic three-state vistas to rocky streams and waterfalls.

If you ride horses, the park offers several horse trails that connect to the popular Virginia Highlands Horse Trail. The park even provides stables for overnight accommodation. A mountain bike trail is available for cyclists.

In addition to the trails and the spectacular views, Grayson Highlands provides insight into what life was like in these mountains generations ago. The human story begins with Eastern Woodland Indians, the Cherokee and Catawba, who camped in the cool spruce forests in summer and hunted the abundant game. Volcanic rock, rhyolite, was used for making stone tools because it held a sharp edge when flicked.

Scots-Irish pioneers came in the late 1700s and settled. They built cabins, hunted and trapped, and farmed on a small scale. Interpretive displays of cabins, rail fences, and quilts demonstrate the craftsmanship of these settlers.

At the visitor center, pioneer life is re-created through displays of furniture, tools, musical instruments, and even a still.

But it is the remoteness of Grayson Highlands, the wildness and incredible natural beauty, that draws most visitors. The great fir and spruce forests here were cut in the early 1900s to provide lumber for a growing America, and it is a tribute to the healing powers of nature that we can hike these mountain trails today and feel as though we are in a wild and untouched landscape.

The hills are alive.

Grayson Highlands at a Glance

GETTING THERE

Grayson Highlands State Park is on U.S. Route 58 west of Galax and south of Marion in Grayson County.

STAYING THERE

Overnight camping is available at the park. Lodging, restaurants, grocery shopping, and medical assistance are available in Galax and Marion.

WANT TO KNOW MORE?

A guide to the park is available from the Department of Conservation and Recreation, 203 Governor Street, Suite 302, Richmond, VA 23219. For information on park programs, including hikes and interpretive programs led by park staff, call the park at 276-579-7092. Or visit the Web site at http://www.dcr.state.va.us.

Hellbent on Salamanders

In the mountains of southwest Virginia, a hunt for salamanders leaves no stone unturned

Gregory McConnell has made a career of finding slimy things under rotten logs and rocks. McConnell, a professor of biology at Emory and Henry College, is an expert on salamanders, those slick little creatures that live in places where the sun doesn't shine.

McConnell led a group of Nature Conservancy members on a salamander hunt a while back, and, since no one in our family had ever been face-to-face with a salamander, we decided it would be an enlightening way to spend a spring Saturday.

The occasion was the annual meeting of the Nature Conservancy of Virginia, held in Abingdon, which is famous for two things: the Barter Theatre and a wonderfully diverse population of salamanders. According to McConnell, some two dozen species can be found in southwest Virginia, from the huge hellbender, which can grow to two feet or more in length, to the tiny and elusive pigmy salamander, usually found in mountainous terrain above four thousand feet.

McConnell said we'd go big-game salamander hunting first, so we drove from Abingdon to Damascus, parked at the little-league field, and waded into Beaver Dam Creek in search of the hellbender. The hellbender is by reputation a mean and ugly critter, about as slick and slimy as they come. A lot of folks think they're poisonous, but they're not. "When people come across one, they're hellbent on getting away from it. That's how it got its name," McConnell said.

McConnell, dressed in a tie-dyed Emory and Henry T-shirt and red bandana, lifted the edge of a small rock and came up with a tiny salamander, an unidentifiable juvenile. "This is the hot spot in the world for salamanders," he said. "The geography of the area isolated many populations, then genetic differences built up, and new species evolved. The salamanders we have here are unique in that they are the only invertebrate animals that have neither gills nor lungs. They breathe through their skin, and that's why they need a moist environment."

Volunteer Rod Miller lifted another rock. McConnell scooped under it with a fine net and this time came up empty. After an hour on Beaver Dam Creek, we had found a few juvenile salamanders, a small water snake, a chub, a darter, and a crawfish carrying a scarlet egg mass, but no hellbenders. "It's hit or miss," said McConnell. "Let's go look for terrestrials."

Terrestrials are salamanders that live in damp places on land. They can be found under rotting logs and rocks, and the hunting is especially good after a rain, McConnell told us. We drove from Damascus out U.S. Route 58 to Whitetop Mountain, the second-tallest in Virginia, and began hiking a trail through a hardwood forest that had been logged probably in the thirties. There were plenty of small, flat rocks on the ground, as well as fallen limbs. Prime salamander habitat, said McConnell.

The first find was made by young Colin Williams, a budding biologist yet in elementary school. "Oh, you got a good one," said McConnell. "See the little brassy flecks on its back? That tells you it's a Weller's. These are found only on mountaintops in southwest Virginia, northeast Tennessee, and northwest North Carolina."

McConnell dampened the salamander with water as we examined it. "The Weller's is a high-altitude salamander," said McConnell. "So it lives in a very stressful environment, and food can be hard to come by. All salamanders are carnivorous, and these small ones feed on small invertebrates. At this altitude, the food source can be limited, and many species breed only every other year because of the high energy demands."

On our way up the mountain, we found several other Weller's salamanders, plus redbacks and Jordan's salamanders.

Our group must have presented a humorous spectacle to other weekend hikers on Whitetop. There were about fifteen of us, ranging in age from perhaps eight to seventy, fanned out through the woods, prying out rocks and lifting rotting limbs. Now and then someone would make a find and shout for McConnell, and he'd come hustling along the mountainside in his tie-dyed shirt and red bandana, ready to make an identification.

But as a biologist, McConnell takes salamanders seriously. "Salamanders are indicator species," he told us. "They are a measure of the health of our environment. Most breathe primarily through their skin, so they are very sensitive to pollutants. There has been a lot of concern about the declining population of frogs worldwide, and the same thing is going on with salamanders. No one really knows why. Some blame toxins in the environment, global warming, or ultraviolet radiation.

"The golden toad of Costa Rica was once plentiful, and within five years it became extinct. We found that the average temperature on the mountain range where it lived rose each year during that period, and the species that lived in the lower elevations began moving up the mountain to a cooler environment. Eventually, the animals that lived at the top level were displaced, and the golden toad, I'm afraid, is out of here."

Such instances remind us that frogs, toads, salamanders, and humans all share the same environment. If they fare well, we fare well.

Salamanders at a Glance

WHAT SPECIES IS IT?

Greg McConnell's favorite field guide to salamanders is the *Peterson Field Guide to Reptiles and Amphibians of Eastern/Central North America*. The Virginia Department of Game and Inland Fisheries has published an *Atlas of Amphibians and Reptiles of Virginia* (Mitchell and Reay, 1999), which is available for $7.50 from the Richmond headquarters of the department. Information is also available on the department Web site: www.dgif.state.va.us.

WHERE CAN I FIND THEM?

Most salamanders have no gills or lungs, and so they breathe primarily through their skin. They look for moist environments such as streambeds and swamps, and they often hide under rocks and rotting logs. The best way to find and identify salamanders is to go with an expert. There are several naturalist rallies through the summer in various areas. The Mount Rogers Naturalist Rally is held each May. Roan Mountain has several rallies with field trips.

BE CAREFUL WITH THEM

Salamanders must remain moist in order to breathe. Return them to their homes as quickly as possible. McConnell recommends that if you remove one from under a rock or log, place it next to the rock or log when you release it. It will find its way back. If you move rocks or logs, return them to their original position.

The Virginia Creeper Trail

A thirty-four-mile bike ride, and nearly all downhill

It was 1991, and Phoebe Cartwright was sick of the business world. Based in Chapel Hill, North Carolina, Cartwright spent much of her time on the road selling specialty food products. Cartwright had grown up in southwest Virginia near Bristol and longed to get back to the rolling mountains of the Blue Ridge.

So Cartwright moved to the town of Damascus, bought a house, and purchased a much-used van from the Methodist church. She then designed and built a bicycle trailer to tow behind the van, and thus began Blue Blaze Shuttle Service, specializing in transporting bike riders to the summit of Whitetop Mountain.

Whitetop Mountain is the southern terminus of the Virginia Creeper Trail, a 34.3-mile former railroad right-of-way that runs from Whitetop to Damascus to Abingdon. The last train chugged along the Creeper Trail in March 1977, and Norfolk and Western Railroad soon after sold the rails as scrap. The U.S. Forest Service bought the right-of-way, and in 1986 Congress designated the Creeper as a National Recreation Trail.

Since then, bicyclists from around the region have discovered that the Creeper Trail provides a ride like few other bike trails in the eastern United States. From Whitetop to Damascus the Creeper runs through the Jefferson National Forest, crossing wooden trestles, running through thickets of rhododendron and mountain laurel, and for much of its length accompanying Whitetop Laurel Creek, a fine little trout stream.

The town of Damascus prospered in the early 1900s because of the timber and iron ore industries and because of the narrow-gauge railroad that got these raw materials to market. But when the iron ore petered out and all the accessible timber was cut, the railroad, and the town, fell on hard times.

Ironically, the rail line Norfolk and Western abandoned when it became unprofitable is now the key to the economic resurgence of Damascus. When Lynn and I visited recently, the town looked clean and prosperous. The older homes had been restored, and the shops along Main Street seemed to be doing a brisk business.

In addition to the Creeper Trail, the Appalachian Trail runs through town, making Damascus a focal point for both hikers and bikers. When we took the Blue Blaze shuttle to Whitetop, the driver said Damascus likes to think of itself as the trail capital of the east and the friendliest town on the trail. He pointed out a hostel operated by the church, where hikers and bikers can find a bunk for four dollars a night. "If they don't have four dollars, they'll give them the lawn mower and a rake and let them earn it," he said.

Tom Horsch runs Adventure Damascus Bicycles, a retail bike shop and one of three Damascus shuttle services that cater to riders of the Creeper Trail. "Five trails run through Damascus, and the economic impact they bring is huge," said Horsch. "The forest service estimates that the Creeper Trail alone brings in a hundred thousand people a year. The Appalachian Trail is probably the best known, but the Creeper Trail probably brings in more people who come for weekend recreation."

In addition to the Creeper and Appalachian Trails, Damascus is on the TransAmerica '76 bike route, which runs from Yorktown to Oregon, and on the Iron Mountain Trail, which runs the length of the Mount Rogers National Recreation Area. The Daniel Boone Heritage Trail, a scenic driving trail that approximates the route Boone took through the Cumberland Gap, also comes through town.

"The trails have had an obvious economic impact on the town,

but I think as much as anything they've given Damascus an iden-
tity," said Horsch. "They've given us a chance to showcase our community as being a friendly small American town, which is what we
are and what we want to be."

John Reese left the world of newspaper advertising five years ago
to open a bed-and-breakfast business in Damascus. He also is chair-
man of the town's parks and recreation commission. Reese, like
Horsch, is gambling that an industry centered on hiking and biking
will pay dividends.

"The trails have been good for business," he said, "and Tom
(Horsch) and Phoebe Cartwright have had a lot to do with that. The
trails have been here for quite some time, but I don't think anyone
realized the potential they offered. And then, about ten years ago,
Phoebe began a shuttle service, taking riders up Whitetop. The pop-
ularity of the trails began growing after that. Now we have three
businesses that provide shuttle service, plus hiking supplies businesses, bed-and-breakfasts, restaurants, and weekend rentals."

The natural landscape is the draw, Reese says. "We're surrounded
by national forest on three sides, and some people might think that's
a downer because it limits growth, but I think that provides value.
Unless someone figures out a way to roll up the mountains, I don't
have to worry about it. The mountains are the reason people will
come here."

Route 58 from Damascus to Whitetop is an asphalt roller-coaster,
two lanes of hairpin turns and switchbacks that run along some of
the highest country in Virginia. Nearby is Mount Rogers, which at
5,729 feet is the highest point in the commonwealth.

We climbed for nearly the entire drive from Damascus to Whitetop, and soon after we got on the trail we realized why cyclists prefer
to bike from Whitetop to Damascus, and not the other way around.
Whitetop stands at about 3,575 feet, and Damascus is at 1,930. So
the eighteen-mile ride is nearly all downhill, but gently so.

Given the downhill gradient, the temptation is to speed through
the trail, but to do so would mean missing out on some spectacular
scenery. The Creeper Trail crosses a hundred wooden trestles as it
makes its way toward Abingdon, and nearly all of them offer a view.
Some are only a few dozen feet long and span a modest tumbling

stream, but others, such as the South Holston Lake trestle, are more than five hundred feet long.

Much of the trail also runs along or crosses rocky streams. When we visited, heavy rains had swollen the small creeks, and Whitetop Laurel Creek had the look of a major whitewater river. There are many places along the trail where you can stop for a streamside lunch or simply stretch your legs for a few minutes.

The Whitetop-to-Damascus portion of the trail is probably the most popular with cyclists. Most of it runs through U.S. Forest Service land, and the downhill grade makes it an easy ride for young riders or beginners.

The trail from Damascus to Abingdon crosses private property and is a bit more attached to civilization, although the section around South Holston Lake offers a spectacular view. Close to Abingdon, the trail skirts a golf course and a major housing development and actually goes uphill slightly for the last few miles.

Since Phoebe Cartwright's return to the Virginia Highlands, her business has grown as more people have learned about the charms of the Creeper Trail. "When I started out, I thought, 'Okay, this will feed me.' I had no idea how it would grow. When I bought eight rental bikes, everyone thought I had lost my mind," she says.

But now Cartwright's fleet stands at fifty bicycles, and the old church van has been replaced by a new model and supplemented by a small bus. In the summer, she and her drivers will shuttle three hundred cyclists a week to the summit of Whitetop, and on the descent many of them will realize why Cartwright decided a decade ago to give up life in the big city and return to these hills.

The Virginia Creeper Trail at a Glance

GETTING THERE

Damascus is on U.S. Route 58 approximately fifteen miles southeast of Abingdon in Washington County. Blue Blaze Shuttle Service (800-475-5095) and Adventure Damascus Tours (888-595-2453) in Damascus provide bicycle rentals and shuttle service to Whitetop and will pick you up at Abingdon if you choose to ride the entire 34.3 miles.

RIDING THE TRAIL

The trail is hard-packed clay and gravel, making it more suitable for mountain bikes than road bikes. Some sections can be muddy and slippery after a rain. The trail is also open to hikers and horseback riders. Trail etiquette calls for cyclists to signal when passing pedestrians, and cyclists should not enter a trestle when an equestrian is on it.

STAYING THERE

Abingdon offers a number of bed-and-breakfast establishments, motels, and the famous Martha Washington Inn. Abingdon has a revitalized downtown, with antiques shops, fine dining, and the Barter Theatre. Contact the Abingdon Convention and Visitors Bureau at 800-435-3440 for more information, or visit the Web site at www .abingdon.com/tourism.

Warblers in the Mist

*Searching for birds in the
Virginia Highlands*

On the map, the road up Brumley Mountain in southwest Virginia looks like a chain of paper clips. With each sharp turn it ascends at a dizzying rate, and by the time we reached four thousand feet the car was wheezing and sputtering. We pulled over when we noticed the ominous aroma of engine parts overheating, so the car stayed where it was and we continued on foot.

I loaded my fanny pack with the camera, a bird guide, microcassette recorder, and a bottle of peach-flavored tea; put the binoculars around my neck; and we continued onward and upward—my wife, Lynn; son, Tom; and me. Tom is built for climbing mountains—all feet, legs, arms, and sinew. Lynn and I, however, are possessed of considerably more avoirdupois. Gravity does not treat us kindly. So as Tom raced ahead, Lynn and I followed at a deliberate pace, pausing often to look for warblers in spruce thickets.

On this particular morning, Brumley Mountain was cloaked in the blue mist that gives the Blue Ridge Mountains their name. As we climbed, the road became rutted and rocky, and it disappeared into the mist a short distance ahead of us. On the mountain, well removed from the nearest traffic, it was quiet and still save for the sound of songbirds, which seemed to be everywhere. The mist and the singing of the birds gave the mountain an ethereal quality. We could not see where we were going or where we had been, and the songs of the birds seemed amplified by the quiet and confining mist.

Mainly there were indigo buntings, probably hundreds of them along the two-mile trail we hiked. The males would perch on the tops of spruce snags and sing with their heads tilted back. Now and then we would see a brightly colored male foraging along the trail with his dull brown mate.

But we had not come up Brumley Mountain to see buntings; we wanted warblers, specifically the high-country warblers one finds above three thousand feet—Canada warblers, black-throated greens and blues, chestnut-sided, northern parulas.

We had been birding in the Virginia Highlands before, but it had always been a secondary activity to a business trip or family vacation—an hour or two on a hiking trail, an afternoon spent patrolling the back roads. We decided to go specifically for the birds, especially the songbirds that would be breeding in the remote mountains of southwest Virginia in May and June.

It is an immensely productive area for songbirds. For many songbirds that nest in the northern U.S. and Canada, the summer range maps typically show a finger that extends southward along the Blue Ridge chain of the Appalachian Mountains through Virginia and into North Carolina, West Virginia, and eastern Kentucky and Tennessee. Indeed, on a clear day, you can stand on a peak in the highlands of southwest Virginia and see all five states.

On advice from friends who live in the area, we selected four different areas to explore over a three-day trip, providing us with a range of habitats and elevations, meaning we would have a chance to see not only high-country birds such as chestnut-sided warblers, but Kentucky warblers, ovenbirds, black-and-white warblers, yellow warblers, vireos, and others more commonly found at the lower to intermediate levels.

The four areas we picked were Hidden Valley Wildlife Management Area (WMA) on Brumley Mountain, Clinch Mountain WMA, Grayson Highlands State Park/Mount Rogers National Recreation Area, and the Virginia Creeper Trail, a thirty-four-mile former railroad bed that runs from the Mount Rogers area to the town of Abingdon. All are within a radius of about thirty-five miles from Abingdon.

We picked Brumley Mountain for our first trip probably because it represents such a departure from the habitat we are used to. We live on the Virginia coast, where anything more than fifty feet above sea level is considered high elevation. Brumley is truly high and wild, with one of the southernmost stands of red spruce on the east coast. It has a sixty-acre lake at the thirty-six-hundred-foot level, and most of the tract is wooded. At the top of the mountain is a communications tower operated by a cellular phone company.

We first hiked up the service road to the tower complex, and when we reached the peak we could see only halfway up the tower because of the mist. But we did see birds, and hear birds, all along the trail. The first was a northern parula—heard and not seen—

somewhere off in the mist. The song is similar to that of a prairie warbler—a trill that rises in pitch—but it ends with an abrupt "zit."

The first highland warbler we saw was a black-throated blue. Even in the mist the bird was readily identifiable, with its black throat and sides, white belly, and bold white patch at the base of the primaries. I use a microcassette recorder to take notes when I'm hiking—a notepad and pencil are too clumsy, and I have no ability to sketch—and I described the bird, its habitat, and the elevation; and I recorded its song.

By mid-morning the mist was clearing, and we discovered what for us was the prize of the day, a male chestnut-sided warbler, which we rarely see on the coast. It was a male in breeding plumage—yellow crown, black eye line and whiskers, chestnut on the flanks—a handsome little bird.

On the way down we spotted a large bird thrashing about in the underbrush, and, as we approached, it accommodated us nicely by perching on the lower branch of an oak. It was a rufous-sided towhee, a male, and when I clicked on the recorder it cooperated further by repeating its call note, "tow-WHEE," several times.

The thick forest was alive with birdsong—the equivalent of the "personals" column in the newspaper. Male indigo bunting seeking female, age unimportant, must like beetles, weevils, and dandelion seeds. . . .

There were other songs we could not identify, and by the time we returned to the car we had persuaded ourselves to invest in a cassette set of bird songs the next time we were in a birding shop.

We returned to Hidden Valley Lake and had lunch along the shore, accompanied by a pair of mallards. Along the wooded western shore of the pond, wood ducks had taken up a nesting box provided by the Department of Game and Inland Fisheries, which manages the WMA. A female ruffed grouse emerged from a roadside thicket with her brood of chicks.

Clinch Mountain WMA

Clinch Mountain is one of Virginia's largest state-owned wildlife management areas. It is located approximately fifteen miles northeast of Hidden Valley, and as part of the Appalachian chain it is high, rugged territory with crests of more than forty-five hundred feet.

A well-maintained service road follows Laurel Bed Creek along the slopes of Clinch Mountain, ending at three-hundred-acre Laurel Bed Lake. Small, rocky streams are abundant, and Big Tumbling Creek, which joins Laurel Bed Creek, is a popular trout stream.

Birds vary according to season and elevation, but the list of nesting songbird species is impressive. It includes our largest warbler, the yellow-breasted chat, the hooded warbler, common yellowthroat, black-and-white warbler, and Louisiana waterthrush, among many others. In the higher elevations are Canada warblers, black-throated greens and blues, chestnut-sided, solitary vireos, and veerys. Indigo buntings seem to be abundant at all elevations. The high, open areas are great for observing the fall hawk migration, and the nearby Mendota Fire Tower is widely used for this purpose.

The well-maintained service roads of Clinch Mountain WMA make it popular for those who want to see birds but are unable or unwilling to tackle the steep slopes by foot. We spent an afternoon there after a morning of rather strenuous hiking at Hidden Valley, so we appreciated the more passive approach to birding the facility afforded. We drove to the summit, stopping often at pullovers to look for birds or to wade in Laurel Bed Creek.

Grayson Highlands/Mount Rogers

Mount Rogers, at 5,729 feet, is the highest point in Virginia. Mount Rogers, Whitetop Mountain, and several other impressive crests are located off Route 58 about twenty-five miles east of Abingdon in an area that includes the Grayson Highlands State Park. These mountainous areas are mentioned often in "Virginia's Birdlife—An Annotated Checklist," published by the Virginia Society of Ornithology, especially with regard to nesting songbirds. The state's peak count of fifty-one Canada warblers, for example, was made at Mount Rogers.

The highlands have breeding populations of Swainson's warblers and northern waterthrushes, representing the northern and southern edges, respectively, of their summer ranges. The Nashville warbler, whose summer range is generally considered southern Canada and the Great Lakes region, is believed to nest in the Mount Rogers area. The magnolia warbler is a common summer resident.

Grayson Highlands State Park is a large, uncrowded natural area featuring numerous amenities, breathtaking views, and an assortment of trails. A campground provides space for tent camping and also water and electric hookups for RVs. A visitor center features interpretive displays on the human history and natural history of the Appalachians.

The park has numerous trails for both hikers and horseback riders, and our favorite is the hike from the visitor center to Twin Pinnacles, rocky outcroppings that afford an expansive view. This spot provides a great vantage point for fall hawk monitoring.

The trail is fairly short at 1.6 miles and is easy to negotiate. It winds through a variety of woodland habitat and emerges at the summit of Haw Orchard Mountain, named for the hawthorn bushes that grow on the mountainside.

As we were walking the trail in early June we heard an unfamiliar bird song and soon located a singing bird perched atop a dead spruce. It was a dark-eyed junco, a bird we are accustomed to seeing in winter on the coast, when it sings rarely if at all. They nest in summer in the higher elevations of the Appalachians, usually above three thousand feet. Soon after, we spotted another breeding bird, a red-eyed vireo, singing in a trailside tree.

The Virginia Creeper Trail

The thirty-four-mile Virginia Creeper Trail connects Abingdon with the Mount Rogers National Recreation Area. It began as an Indian footpath, was later used by European pioneers, and in the early 1900s a railroad was built along it, thus facilitating the removal of timber and iron ore from the mountains. The Creeper made its last run in 1977, and the rail bed is now a hiking/biking trail. It's a great resource for birders, providing access to a wide range of habitats and elevations.

There are more than a dozen access points along the trail, and we began at one at a lower elevation, off Route 677 about four miles east of Abingdon. An old wooden trestle crossed farmland and pasture, and as cattle grazed below us we watched a downy woodpecker bring grubs to her chicks in a cavity in a snag, which was about eye level with us. As the trail entered a forested section we saw a pair of northern orioles foraging along the edge, as well as a pair of northern bobwhites. In the trees along the trail were the ubiquitous indigo buntings.

As we left open land we began to see and hear warblers. A male hooded warbler hunted in a thicket on a hillside, and we spotted a black-throated green warbler in an oak tree. We heard an Acadian flycatcher far back in the woods, and not far away we spotted an eastern wood pewee.

We stopped on a gently curving trestle that crossed a streambed and waited. Soon we heard a common yellowthroat, and a pair of yellow-billed cuckoos flew past. From somewhere in the distance, we heard the loud call of a pileated woodpecker. An American robin foraged for insects in a clearing at the end of the trestle.

The trail curved around the side of the mountain and disappeared into the foliage. Below us a small stream sparkled in a shaft of sunlight. The buntings sang. It was, we agreed, an uncommonly good place to look for birds.

The Virginia Highlands at a Glance

GETTING THERE

Abingdon, just off Interstate 81 twenty miles north of Bristol, is a good focal point for a birding trip in the Highlands. It is a historic, picturesque old town with plenty of antiques shops, restaurants, and other attractions, including the Barter Theatre.

STAYING THERE

Overnight accommodations range from the standard motel chains to numerous bed-and-breakfast establishments. Contact the Abingdon Convention and Visitors Bureau at 800-435-3440 for information or visit the Web site at www.abingdon.com.

WANT TO KNOW MORE?

A good guide to birds of the area is "Virginia's Birdlife, An Annotated Checklist" published by the Virginia Society of Ornithology.

Write VSO Membership Services, 520 Rainbow Forest Drive, Lynchburg, VA 24502 for information. During the nesting season, birds are very vocal, whether they are singing to attract mates or to proclaim territory. It's a good idea to brush up on bird songs before you go. The thick vegetation makes it difficult to get a good look at birds. A microcassette recorder does a remarkable job of picking up bird songs. We record unidentified songs and then sort them out when we return home.

Hungry Mother State Park

A story, perhaps true, adds a bit of legend to the natural landscape of southwest Virginia

During Virginia's frontier days there were numerous skirmishes between Native Americans and European settlers moving westward across the Appalachian Mountains. Some confrontations became part of Virginia's oral history, stories told by one generation to the next, sometimes with a little enhancement.

This story, according to people who should know, is said to be accurate. The setting is a mountainous region along the New River south of what is now the town of Marion. Scots-Irish pioneers had set up a small encampment along the river, hunting and fishing for subsistence while searching for fertile land on which to settle. One day when the men were away from camp, Indians attacked and burned the settlers' cabins and stole whatever goods they could take with them.

In addition to supplies, the Indians also took at least two prisoners, Molly Marley and her young daughter. The Indian party traveled back to their camp farther north along the mountain range, and at some point Molly and her daughter either escaped or were set free in the wilderness. They wandered along a streambed, trying to make their way back south, eating berries to stay alive. Exhausted and starving, Molly eventually collapsed on the bank, and her daughter wandered off in search of help.

Soon after, rescuers found the child, and the only words the little girl could mutter were, "Hungry Mother." When the girl led the men back to the foot of the mountain where she had left her mother, they found Molly dead of starvation. The mountaintop above where she lay became her monument; it was called Molly's Knob. The stream where Molly fell became Hungry Mother Creek. Those names are still on the topo map today.

I hiked up Molly's Knob on a winter morning, thinking about the legend of Molly Marley and her little girl. Rugged country, this. My walk was made considerably more pleasant by a well-maintained trail, but in Molly's day there would have been none. She was probably toughened by the harshness of pioneer life, but as a recent immigrant she likely had few wilderness survival skills. There were berries on the mountainside, but which ones were safe to eat? How did she defend herself against the dangers of the wilderness? How did she keep her child alive?

In the 1930s they dammed Hungry Mother Creek, allowing the water to gently flood the valley and the little hollows where the pioneers once settled, where Native Virginians once hunted. Over time, the stream became a lake—108 acres of prime bass fishing—and an emergency source of water to communities in the region. In keeping with the oral history, they named the lake Hungry Mother, and in 1936 one of Virginia's first six state parks opened here, also named Hungry Mother.

There are rustic cabins, campgrounds, a visitor center and gift shop, a restaurant, and a marina, but there still is something wild about Hungry Mother. I parked the car and took off on Lake Trail, a loop that runs for nearly six miles along a ridge around the lake. In the first half-mile or so there were the usual rustic stone benches, handrails, and timbered steps along steep sections. But then the trail turned left into a hollow and branched off, one path climbing through a series of switchbacks to Molly's Knob, another going back to the lake. Two other trails soon connected with Lake Trail: Middle Ridge, which is something of a backdoor approach to Molly's Knob, and CCC Trail, named for the group of federal workers who built the park in the 1930s.

These trails crisscross the ridges and slopes of the southern portions of Walker Mountain and Little Brushy Mountain, and they are perhaps the best venues for letting your imagination take you back to the day of Molly Marley. On the winter morning when I visited, I stood along the ridge above the lake and watched as a boat came from behind a bend of evergreens. It was a red kayak, paddled by a woman with silver hair. She glided slowly along the shoreline, perhaps watching birds in the lakeside thickets. The water was calm, and the kayak left just a slight wake, punctuated by dimples where the paddle blades had entered the water.

It was a modern boat, made of plastic, but it seemed appropriate there on the lake near where Molly Marley had fallen centuries before. The woman was a strong paddler, and she clearly knew how to handle the boat. She saw me standing on the bluff and waved a paddle blade at me. I waved back, and she went on around the bend, disappearing into a cove lined with evergreens.

Hungry Mother State Park at a Glance

GETTING THERE

Hungry Mother State Park is near the town of Marion in Smyth County. Take Interstate 81 south to Marion. From exit 47 take Johnson Road to U.S. Route 11, turn left, and follow it to Route 16. Turn right and follow Route 16 approximately five miles to the park.

STAYING THERE

The state park has rental cabins and campsites available. Call 800-933-7275 for reservations. For specific information on programs and activities and a map of hiking trails, call the park at 540-781-7400. The town of Marion and the surrounding area have numerous motels, restaurants, and other facilities. Visit the Web site at www .smythcounty.org.

AND WHILE YOU'RE THERE

The Museum of the Middle Appalachians (540-496-3633) is in nearby Saltville. Mount Rogers Recreation Area and Grayson Highlands State Park are south of Marion on Route 16. The drive north on Route 16 will take you through some spectacular mountain scenery to Rich Valley and the town of Tazewell.

Guest River Gorge Trail

It's not Virginia's longest rail-trail, but the views are great

There's something spooky about riding a bicycle through a railroad tunnel. For one thing, it's dark in there. Very dark. And it's damp. And it smells funny. It's not an unpleasant funny smell, just a curious one, like opening a box that has been closed for a long time.

The tunnel on Guest River Gorge Trail is just a short distance from the trailhead, and it comes as something of a surprise when you haven't ridden the trail before and don't know it's there. You're riding along in bright sunshine on a surprisingly warm winter afternoon, and then it's dark and damp and you can't see the trail anymore, only the proverbial light-at-the-end-of-the-tunnel floating out there in the distance. You hope a bear hasn't picked this particular spot for a bit of hibernation.

The rails-to-trails movement is one of the great ideas of our time, especially for those of us who enjoy hiking, biking, and riding horses through some spectacular countryside. It's a concept that makes perfectly good sense. A railroad line has outlived its usefulness, so instead of simply being abandoned, the rail bed is converted to a trail, and the property is donated to the public. The railroad company sells the track as scrap, and it gets a tax write-off. And we get another place to hike or ride without being sucked up in the draft of an eighteen-wheeler.

In many cases, the rail bed needs little more than resurfacing to convert it to a multiple-use trail. The bed is hard-packed from decades of use, trestles and tunnels are in place where needed, and the grade is very gentle, even in mountainous areas, because steam locomotives were not exactly designed for steep climbs.

Virginia has some spectacular trails that once were rail lines. The Virginia Creeper Trail in southwest Virginia is perhaps the most famous and scenic, with dozens of trestles that cross rivers and gorges. The New River Trail near Pulaski runs for more than fifty miles along spectacular whitewater. It was built by the Norfolk and Western Railroad Company to take iron ore out of the mountains, and now it's one of Virginia's newest state parks.

Perhaps Virginia's least-known rails-to-trail park is Guest River Gorge in Scott and Wise Counties. At less than six miles, it's one of the shortest trails, but it rivals the big boys when it comes to natural beauty.

Railroad builders in the late 1800s and early 1900s knew what they were doing. If you're looking for a route to cross a mountain range, you follow the water. If a river has already scoured the way through a sandstone gorge, why build a rail bed elsewhere? It's no accident that most of Virginia's rails-to-trails parks include the sound of rushing water as a sensory perk.

Guest River Gorge Trail begins near the town of Coeburn and runs with the Guest River until its confluence with the Clinch some six miles downstream. At times the trail is near river level, and then the river will drop away, cascading musically over boulders, and fall behind a screen of rhododendron.

I rode the trail recently with Tom Horsch of Damascus, who runs a company that combines outdoor sports such as biking with environmental education. The Guest River Trail is one of Horsch's favorite day trip destinations because it packs a lot of natural beauty into a relatively short ride. It also is uncrowded, as we discovered on our recent weekday ride.

"We have people come to the Creeper Trail from all over the southeast, but the Guest River Gorge Trail has not been discovered yet," said Horsch. "It's a little bit out of the way, so most of the people who use it are local residents."

We parked at the trailhead in the Jefferson National Forest about a mile outside Coeburn, got on our mountain bikes, and headed for the Clinch River. The trail runs slightly downhill here, so the pedaling is easy. The Guest River tumbled along on our right, and on our left was a sandstone cliff perhaps a hundred feet high. We pedaled through a tunnel, over a trestle crossing a side stream, and met our first fellow trail users, two sixtyish men carrying fly rods. The river is stocked with rainbow trout, but the two men had had no luck so far.

Farther along, we met a couple walking their dog, and as the distance from the trailhead increased, we had the Guest River to ourselves for the 5.7-mile ride to the end of the trail. A trestle crosses the Guest where it empties into the Clinch, so Horsch and I parked the bikes, got out the water bottles, and took a break as we watched two modest rivers come together to create one of substance.

Guest River Gorge at a Glance

GETTING THERE

Guest River Gorge Trail is just outside the town of Coeburn in Southwest Virginia. Take Interstate 81 to Abingdon, then take U.S. Route 58 west to Coeburn. Turn left (south) onto Route 72, cross the Guest River, and continue out of town. The trailhead is on the left just past the correctional center.

STAYING THERE

Numerous motels are available in Wise, Norton, Big Stone Gap, Lebanon, and Abingdon. I stayed in Abingdon on a recent trip because it's convenient not only to the Guest River area but also to Damascus, the Virginia Creeper Trail, Grayson Highlands, and other points of interest.

WHILE YOU'RE THERE

Abingdon has several nice restaurants, the Barter Theatre, and numerous antiques shops. Natural Tunnel State Park near Clinchport is worth a visit, as is Hungry Mother State Park near Marion.

Natural Tunnel State Park

What would Daniel Boone have thought?

If it's true what they say, that Daniel Boone was the first white man to see this place, then I'd love to know what he said when he first came across it. I was standing on a rim of a mountain looking down into a place called the Amphitheater, a semicircular basin with rock walls four hundred feet high. At one end of the amphitheater a huge tunnel disappears into the mountain, and it keeps going for more than eight hundred feet.

A railroad track runs through the tunnel now, and if you didn't know better, you'd assume that some Norfolk and Western guys armed with dynamite went to work on it around 1910. But no. This tunnel is the product of a slow process of nature, not the sudden boom of industry.

They say that Boone came across the tunnel when he explored the area in 1775. Boone would probably have reasoned that the tunnel was not built by Norfolk and Western blasters. I wonder what he thought. I suppose he would have returned to camp that evening, gathered his partners together, and begun his story in good Southern fashion: "Now, y'all ain't gonna believe this. . . ."

The tunnel is well below the rim of the mountain, and Boone had to do some scrambling to get down there and back up. I made the climb on a recent visit, but I had it easier than Boone. The tunnel is now protected as part of Natural Tunnel State Park near Duffield in southwest Virginia, and the park folks have thoughtfully built a switchback trail, complete with benches and handrails, for those of us who lack the mountaineering skills of Boone.

Still, it's a steep climb, and once you get down the trail and enjoy the view of the tunnel, you're going to have to make your way back up. That's what the benches are there for. They're not so much rest stops as wheeze stops.

The park also has made life easier for visitors by building a chair-lift running from the mountain rim down into the chasm. It runs only during the busy season of the park, summer through fall, so if you visit during the winter months you can enjoy the trip in and out of the chasm by foot trail.

Natural Tunnel State Park is one of Virginia's most remote parks, and consequently it is a place of great undisturbed beauty. From Abingdon, head west on U.S. Route 58, and just before you get to St. Paul turn left on Route 65. This is a winding two-lane stretch that rambles along the Clinch River, passing country stores, weathered barns, and little churches tucked away in the wildwood.

The state park is just off Route 23 near Duffield. While the park is remote, the facilities are excellent. The park office is a short distance beyond the entrance. A right turn will take you to a parking area where you can hike the trail down to the tunnel or, in season, ride the chairlift into the gorge. There also is a visitor center, a gift shop, an old steam locomotive to explore, and a butterfly garden constructed by Southwest Virginia Master Gardeners.

A left turn at the visitor center (Route 646) will take you over the tunnel past campgrounds, picnic sites, a modern swimming pool complex, and finally to Cove Ridge Center, which, other than the natural amenities, is the star attraction of the park.

Cove Ridge, which opened in 1999, is an environmental education center geared to group retreats, with dormitory facilities for forty-eight guests, a wood-paneled dining room, catering kitchen, and meeting rooms. Park staff conduct classes including insect study, forestry, astronomy, geology, and water testing. For experiences outside the classroom, they will organize canoe trips on the Clinch River or tours of nearby caves.

The real classroom, however, is the park itself, especially if your interests are geology and wildlife. Natural Tunnel is believed to be about a million years old and began forming when carbonic acid in the groundwater slowly dissolved the surrounding limestone and dolomitic bedrock. The hiking path I mentioned leads down to the tunnel, but there are six other trails that lead to mountain overlooks or twist through hollows. Spring Hollow Trail, for example, begins near the park office and runs down to Stock Creek, which helped carve Natural Tunnel.

None of the hiking trails is long—Purchase Ridge Trail is the longest at 1.1 mile—but all offer spectacular views and an opportunity to see the abundant wildlife of the park. They also provide a glimpse of the human history of the area. Before Boone explored these mountains, Native Americans hunted here, and soon after Boone visited, the pioneers settled in. The Carter Family Cabin is located near the south tunnel entrance, and the Amphitheater still bears the scars of Civil War involvement. Confederate soldiers mined saltpeter to make gunpowder, and the excavations can still be seen along the rock walls from the Lover's Leap Overlook.

Natural Tunnel State Park offers a great outdoor experience in one of the most scenic and unexplored parts of Virginia. Daniel Boone left no record of his impression when he visited, but I have a feeling he must have liked the place.

Natural Tunnel at a Glance

GETTING THERE
Natural Tunnel State Park is near the towns of Duffield and Clinchport in Southwest Virginia. From Abingdon take U.S. Route 58 west to Route 65. Follow Route 65 along the Clinch River to Route 23, turn right, and the park entrance will be about a mile down on the right.

STAYING THERE
Overnight accommodations and restaurants are available in Duffield, Gate City, Big Stone Gap, and Wise. Natural Tunnel State Park offers campgrounds, and Cove Ridge Center provides group accommodations with dormitory space for forty-eight. Contact the park at 540-940-2674 for more information.

AND WHILE YOU'RE THERE
The corner of Southwest Virginia has some of the most magnificent natural areas in the state, without the crowds normally associated with such attractions. If you go by way of Route 65, consider return-

ing on Routes 23 and 58, making a loop through Big Stone Gap, Wise, St. Paul, Hansonville, and back to Abingdon. The Southwest Virginia Museum is located near Big Stone Gap, which also is the home of Virginia's state outdoor drama, "The Trail of the Lonesome Pine." High Knob Recreation Area and Guest River Gorge Trail are near Wise.

Other books by Curtis J. Badger

Salt Tide: Cycles and Currents of
Life along the Coast

Bellevue Farm: Exploring
Virginia's Coastal Countryside

A Naturalist's Guide to the
Virginia Coast

Virginia's Eastern Shore: A
Pictorial History

Clams: How to Find, Catch,
and Cook Them

The Barrier Islands